HOODS

The Story of the Ku Klux Klan

by Robert P. Ingalls

G. P. Putnam's Sons · New York

Copyright © 1979 by Robert P. Ingalls
All rights reserved. Published simultaneously in Canada
by General Publishing Co. Limited, Toronto.
Printed in the United States of America
Library of Congress Cataloging in Publication Data
Ingalls, Robert P.
Hoods, the story of the Ku Klux Klan.
Bibliography: p.
Includes index.
Summary: A history of the mysterious hooded organization
from its beginnings during Reconstruction
after the Civil War.
1. Ku-Klux Klan—History—Juvenile literature.
2. Ku-Klux Klan (1915-   )—Juvenile literature.
[1. Ku-Klux Klan—History] I. Title
HS2330.K63I48 1979   322.4'2   78-11596
ISBN 0-399-20658-2
Third impression

For Michèle and Marc

Acknowledgments

My greatest debt in writing this book is to those historians, mentioned in the bibliography, who have done so much to reveal the various activities of the different Klans. Without their work, this book would not have been possible.

The friendly, helpful staff of my publisher made this project an unusually pleasant experience. In particular, I would like to thank Margaret Frith for suggesting the book, Charles Mercer for accepting it, and Anne Hart for improving it.

I would also like to thank my colleagues in the Department of History at the University of South Florida for the support and encouragement they gave me in this project. Steven Lawson took the time to read the entire manuscript, and I appreciate his insightful suggestions that improved the style and analysis at a number of points.

The dedication is to my children, who are a joy in large part due to the efforts of my wife, Joèle, who also performed the invaluable service of keeping the children occupied while I worked on this book.

Contents

1 / The Birth of the Klan

IN THE SPRING OF 1866, A YEAR AFTER THE END OF THE CIVIL WAR, SIX Confederate veterans formed a social club in the town of Pulaski, Tennessee. Bored by peacetime, the young men hoped to find amusement in the secret society they called the "Ku Klux Klan." They took the name from the Greek word *kuklos*, meaning circle. They turned *kuklos* into "Ku Klux" and added the word "Klan" because they liked the sound of "Ku Klux Klan."

This small, harmless and fun-loving group developed into one of the largest, most violent secret organizations in American history. Although the original Klan reached its peak and disappeared within the short span of six years, it left a legendary ritual and tactics that were revived by later generations and continue to haunt America today. The Ku Klux Klan has always sparked controversy. Its supporters have pictured the Klan as a defender of a particular way of life. Opponents have stressed the lawlessness and violence of Klan methods.

Much of the Klan's history is masked in mystery. Because of the order's commitment to secrecy, some basic facts are either unknown or disputed. Even the exact date of the Klan's birth is uncertain. Yet the path followed by the Ku Klux Klan is unmistakable.

The six founders of the Klan were from prominent families of the small town of Pulaski, which lies near the Tennessee border with Alabama. Several of the young veterans were lawyers, and one was an editor for the town's only newspaper. To amuse themselves, the founding Klansmen created an elaborate ritual based on that of college fraternities. The officers included the Grand Cyclops (president), Grand Magi (vice president), and Grand Exchequer (treasurer). The Klansmen adopted a uniform of a white mask, a high pointed hat, and a long robe.

Despite its secrecy, the Ku Klux Klan was originally designed for fun and differed little from similar societies. For about a year a small number of Klansmen in Pulaski and the surrounding area simply initiated new members and enjoyed the companionship offered by the social club.

During that time, the Republican-controlled Congress spelled out its program for reconstructing former Confederate states. Following on the heels of the abolition of slavery, Congressional Reconstruction required that Southern states extend legal and political rights to all blacks, including former slaves. Under the first federal civil rights law and the Fourteenth Amendment to the Constitution, blacks were made full citizens of the United States, and states were prohibited from denying any citizen life, liberty, or equal protection under the law. This meant that for the first time former slaves could own property, make contracts, and exercise other fundamental rights on the same basis as whites. In addition, Congress gave black men the right to vote and hold public office.

Adopted during 1866-67, the Republican party's Reconstruction program threatened to turn southern society upside down. The promise of equal rights for blacks flew in the face of the widely held opinion of white Southerners that the black race was innately inferior. This deep-seated racist belief had served to justify slavery, and it remained a major obstacle to uplifting blacks after the Civil War. Indeed, antiblack hatred drove some whites to take extreme measures to resist Reconstruction.

Tennessee had become the first Southern state to give black men, including recently freed slaves, the right to vote. With the Republican party controlling the state government and blacks starting to exercise newly won freedoms, ex-Confederates began to take up arms to oppose Reconstruction. Intimidation and violence were increasingly used against blacks and their white supporters in the Republican party.

As Tennessee changed, so too did the Ku Klux Klan. A year after its creation, the onetime social club joined the rising campaign against Republican Reconstruction. The new direction of the Klan was planned and well organized. In the spring of 1867, delegates from Klan groups in Tennessee were called to Nashville by Pulaski's Grand Cyclops. The gathering adopted a "Prescript," or constitution, which created an elaborate organizational structure permitting the Klan to spread across the South. In addition to the local Grand Cyclops, there was now a state organization headed by the Grand Dragon, and at the peak of the pyramid stood the Grand Wizard of the Empire. The top post went to General Nathan Bedford Forrest, a dashing Confederate cavalry officer. The Prescript set an initiation fee of $1 for new members, but bodies soon proved more important than money in Klan recruiting. New members had to be over eighteen and recommended by a Klansman. Sworn to secrecy, recruits pledged to "protect the weak, the innocent, and the defenseless, from the indignities, wrongs, and outrages of the lawless, the violent, and the brutal."

In practice these thinly veiled goals meant a Klan defense of white supremacy. The targets of the Klan were not simply common criminals but rather northern Republicans and blacks who threatened the tradition of white dominance. The originators of the Klan crusade against Reconstruction apparently thought their ends could be achieved nonviolently, but they were quickly disappointed.

Despite the highly centralized plan for expanding the Ku Klux Klan, the secret order spread so rapidly that most chapters operated independently. As the founders lost control of the Klan, it became impossible to talk about a single Ku Klux Klan. Yet Klan activities followed a common pattern throughout the post–Civil War South.

After its reorganization in 1867, the Klan first spread across Tennessee. Except for the eastern part of the state, where the Confederate cause had always been unpopular, the Ku Klux Klan found widespread support in the Volunteer State. At first, Klansmen used tricks in their attempt to keep blacks "in their place." Riding through the night, white-robed, hooded Klansmen tried to fool blacks into thinking ghosts were after them. However, masked Klansmen quickly turned from harmless pranks to more violent means of suppressing blacks. Klan leaders proved unable to control their many followers, and the nonviolent intimidation of blacks and their white supporters degenerated into a lawless reign of terror. Although the violence was often random and arbitrary, there was method in the apparent madness. The victims of Klansmen were almost always black or, if white, associated with the hated Republican party.

Typically, hooded Klansmen invaded the homes of blacks at night to avenge real or imagined misdeeds. The alleged wrongs committed by blacks included everything from insulting whites to voting for Republicans, but political activity was the most common offense. For this perfectly legal action, blacks were whipped, beaten, shot, and killed. Floggings could mean hundreds of lashes with a whip and permanent scars. Blacks who tried to resist were most likely to wind up dead. Night-riding Klansmen often forced blacks to promise that they would not vote for Republican candidates. Since the secret ballot was not used, voting was easily monitored by Klansmen.

The Klan's political emphasis also led to threats and attacks against white Republicans, particularly those who were public officials. Directed at Republican "carpetbaggers" who came from the North and southern "scalawags" who cooperated with them, the Klan's campaign of terror was designed to keep them from getting elected and to force their resignation if they won.

Fears of black equality frequently sparked Klan attacks on schools set up for freed slaves. Klansmen warned blacks not to attend school, and masked men forced teachers, many of them from out of state, to leave town.

In some cases, Klansmen charged blacks with crimes such as arson or rape. But the Klan vigilantes broke the law by setting themselves up as judge and jury without the need for proof. They then summarily punished alleged criminals on the spot with a whipping or lynching. However, Klansmen were less concerned with upholding the criminal code than with enforcing white supremacy. In fact, Klan victims were most frequently accused of activities like voting that were completely legal.

The outrages committed by the Klan troubled some of its founders. In an anonymous letter to newspapers, one of the founders declared: "It is to be lamented that the simple object of the original Ku-Kluxes should be so perverted as to become political and pernicious in its demonstrations. If it has become an organization with guerilla and 'lynch-law' attributes, then better the Ku Klux had never been heard of, and the sooner such organization is dissolved, the better for the country at large—especially for the South."

Despite this warning from one of the six original Klansmen, the society's brand of lynch law proved so popular that it was copied throughout the South. In the wake of the Klan's reign of terror in Tennessee, the secret order spread in 1868 to every former Confederate state, from Virginia to Texas. As in Tennessee, the Klan's growth was ignited by the enforcement of Reconstruction, which extended legal rights, especially the vote, to blacks.

The Klan's recruiting campaign was aided by the Grand Wizard, General Nathan Bedford Forrest, who took the Klan's message into the Deep South. Newspapers sympathetic to the Democratic party also spread the word about this new antiblack and anti-Republican organization. Many groups calling themselves Ku Kluxers were organized locally with no affiliation with the original Klan in Tennessee. Yet the Klan was commonly referred to as "the Invisible Empire," which increased its aura of mystery and gave the impression it was a single, unified group.

However and wherever Klansmen appeared in the South, they followed the pattern set by the Tennessee Klan. The uniform varied somewhat, but masked and robed Klansmen shattered the calm of southern nights as they took to their horses and went about their serious and hateful business. Most often this meant a raid on a black family isolated somewhere in the rural South. Taken by surprise in the dead of night and hopelessly outnumbered, Klan victims were at the mercy of their tormentors.

As in Tennessee, Klansmen in other states quickly turned from nonviolent threats to terror. At first, the Klan might just post printed warnings around town, but those were soon backed up by violence. In Georgia, a mob of masked men murdered George W. Ashburn, a white Republican who was active in state politics. The Klan's campaign of terror peaked during the election campaign of 1868, when the purpose of the violence was clearly to defeat Republicans and elect Democrats. Thousands of blacks and white Republicans fell victim not only to beatings but also to murder. In Arkansas, over 200 people, including a U.S. congressman, were killed in the three months before the 1868 election. Most of the crimes went unsolved, but their political nature made them

13

unmistakably the work of vigilantes, many of whom called themselves Klansmen.

When the wave of violence continued after the election, some Klan leaders tried to stem the tide. In 1869, the Grand Wizard of the Ku Klux Klan, General Forrest, ordered Klansmen to restrict their activities. Claiming that the original purpose of the Klan had been perverted by undesirable members, General Forrest demanded that Klansmen give up their masks and disguises. The Grand Wizard also barred threatening letters, whippings, and interference with political activities. Although General Forrest's order was disregarded by many Klansmen, it amounted to an admission that the Klan had become a terrorist group.

Revulsion against the Klan by many of its former supporters led to its official disbandment. The Klan's Tennessee leaders formally dissolved the group in 1869. The Ku Klux Klan did not disappear, but henceforth General Forrest and other former Klan leaders could wash their hands of any violence and blame it on renegade Klan members.

In many areas of the South, Klansmen paid no attention to the order to disband, and the campaign of terror continued. The Carolinas, Georgia, and Alabama saw some of the worst mob violence in 1869 and 1870. In most cases, Klansmen lashed out at blacks, but they also attacked a few whites associated with Republican Reconstruction. In York County, South Carolina, one group of Klan members numbering some 2,000 men was responsible for a reign of terror that left 11 people dead and over 600 others whipped or beaten. Five black schools and churches were also destroyed.

When local governments proved unable or unwilling to stop the Klan's violent actions, the federal government finally stepped in. Beginning in 1870, Congress passed a series of laws, including the Ku Klux Klan Act of 1871, that made it a federal crime for anyone to deprive citizens of their constitutional rights. Congressional investigations and mounting complaints about Klan terrorism gradually brought enforcement of the federal laws. Although Democrats still denied that the Ku Klux Klan was a problem, Republican officials started prosecuting Klansmen in federal court. Large-scale arrests and a few convictions led to a sudden decline in the Klan's terrorism. In some cases, convictions were obtained through the testimony of Klansmen who pleaded guilty and then informed on others. By the end of 1872, the federal crackdown had broken the back of the Ku Klux

Klan. Violence directed largely at blacks continued to plague the South, but only in isolated instances was it the work of masked night riders calling themselves Klansmen.

Long after its death, the Reconstruction Klan lived on in southern legend. Its opposition to black equality and Republican rule made the Ku Klux Klan appear a heroic defender of "the southern way of life" in the eyes of many law-abiding whites who never joined the Klan but still despised Reconstruction. It was this legendary Klan that most Southerners would remember, rather than the very real gangs of terrorists who broke the law by beating, shooting, and murdering both blacks and whites.

2 / The Klan Rides Again

ON THANKSGIVING NIGHT, 1915, SIXTEEN MEN FROM ATLANTA, GEORGIA, climbed to the top of nearby Stone Mountain. Led by "Colonel" William Joseph Simmons, they braved the cold, windy weather to join in a solemn ceremony.

The small group first built an altar of stones on which they placed an American flag, a Bible, and a sword. Then they erected a wooden cross sixteen feet high and set it on fire. In the eerie light of the burning cross, the sixteen men "solemnly dedicated themselves, as Americans, to those principles of Americanism embodied in the Constitution of the United States, consecrated themselves, as Protestants, to the tenets of the Christian religion, and pledged themselves, as white men, to the eternal maintenance of white supremacy."

A week later, this group applied for and received a state charter making it "the Knights of the Ku-Klux Klan, Inc." Modeled after the organization that had terrorized the South during Reconstruction, the new Klan attracted little attention. In time, however, it became the largest, most powerful Klan in history.

The moving spirit behind the revival of the Ku Klux Klan was William Joseph Simmons. Born in a small Alabama town in 1880, he grew up in a period when Reconstruction and the original Klan were still fresh in the minds of Southerners.

"My father was an officer of the old Klan in Alabama back in the 60's," Simmons later recalled. "I was always fascinated by Klan stories. I heard my dad tell them. . . . My old Negro mammy, Aunt Viney, and her husband, Uncle George, used to tell us children about how the old Reconstruction Klansmen used to frighten the darkies."

In 1898, at eighteen, Simmons joined the army to fight in the Spanish-American War. During the brief war he never rose above his original rank of private.

After the war, young Simmons served as minister for the Methodist church. Riding the circuit in Florida and Alabama, he drew people to revival meetings with sermon titles like "Red Heads, Dead Heads, and No Heads." "And just to show you how much I had the old Ku Klux Klan on my mind," Simmons later said, "I had another lecture which I called 'Kinship of Kourtship and Kissing'—three K's, you see—and that was 'way back ten years before I started the Klan."

Yet Simmons failed to get a large church of his own. Disappointed and troubled by mounting debts, he looked elsewhere for fame and fortune.

In 1912, the ex-preacher turned to recruiting for fraternal organizations. Like many fellow Americans, Simmons was a "joiner." He belonged to a number of men's social clubs, including the Masons, the Knights of Pythias, the Odd Fellows, and the Woodmen of the World.

"I have been a fraternalist ever since I was in the academy school way back yonder," Simmons once declared. "I believe in fraternal orders and fraternal relationships among men."

As a professional organizer for such groups, Simmons quickly achieved financial success. "Within two years," he bragged, "I had a little home worth $3,000, all paid for. All my debts had been settled and I was in Atlanta earning $15,000 a year as district manager for a national fraternal order." With this position in the Woodmen of the World went the honorary title "Colonel," which Simmons proudly carried for the rest of his life.

Outwardly, he looked like he might really have been a southern colonel. Standing over six feet, he appeared every inch a gentleman with his square jaw, thin lips, and spacious forehead. His prominent nose was balanced by spectacles and bushy eyebrows. He had a strong, well-rounded voice, and he spoke slowly and deliberately like a man of position and authority.

His success as a leader of the Woodmen nourished his great dream of creating his own fraternal order. A twist of fate in the form of an automobile accident gave Simmons the opportunity to develop his scheme.

"During three months in bed I planned the Klan," he later recalled. "I planned the robes and the pointed helmet and the mask. I worked out all the emblems and all the ritual." All this he carefully copyrighted in his own name so that no one else could form a competing Klan.

Colonel Simmons then set out to find followers among lodge members in Atlanta. His recruiting campaign coincided with the release of a new movie that depicted the rise of the original Ku Klux Klan during Reconstruction. The movie, *Birth of a Nation*, had perhaps the greatest impact on America of any film ever made.

The screenplay for *Birth of a Nation* was based loosely on a best-selling novel, *The Clansman*. Written by Thomas Dixon, Jr., in 1905, the melodramatic story represented the Ku Klux Klan as the savior of the South during the years following the Civil War. For Dixon, the threat to white civilization supposedly came from recently freed slaves, whom he portrayed as savage wild beasts.

Dixon turned his book into a play that toured the country with phenomenal success, especially in the South. One drama critic compared the impact of the play to that of a "runaway car loaded with dynamite." Another called *The Clansman* "the greatest theatrical triumph in the history of the South." One dissenter, however, found it "disgusting."

In the search for wider audiences, Dixon decided to make a motion picture of his story. This was at a time when the movie industry was just getting its start. Techniques for the silent motion picture were primitive, and many people did not consider it a serious art form.

All this was changed by D. W. Griffith, a young director, who turned *The Clansman* into a sweeping epic film that ran for two hours and forty-five minutes—an unheard of length. Dixon was so overwhelmed by the scope and emotional impact of the movie that he changed the title to *Birth of a Nation*. Yet the film seemed doomed, since its controversial subject matter generated immediate opposition to its showing.

In hopes of avoiding possible suppression of the film by local censors, Dixon took a series of bold steps early in 1915. First, he asked an old friend from college days, President Woodrow Wilson, to preview the movie. Wilson agreed, and after a private showing in the White House, the president declared: "It is like writing history with lightning."

Then Dixon got the Supreme Court of the United States to see the movie. The Chief Justice, Edward Douglass White from Louisana, at first rejected the idea of looking at anything as vulgar as a moving picture, but he agreed as soon as he learned the subject of the film. "I was a member of the Klan," Chief Justice White told Dixon.

With this kind of semiofficial backing, *Birth of a Nation* escaped suppression and opened to the public in March, 1915. The film became an immediate hit, selling out a New York theater for 280 consecutive performances and running for forty-seven straight weeks. Similar crowds flocked to see the sensational movie in cities across the country.

Birth of a Nation also generated an enormous furor because of its antiblack stereotypes. Oswald Garrison Villard, a prominent journalist, called the film a "deliberate attempt to humiliate 10,000,000 American citizens and portray them as nothing but beasts." Booker T. Washington, the black educator widely recognized as the spokesman for American blacks, denounced the movie.

Public showings of *Birth of a Nation* sparked protests and violence in the North. One spectator threw eggs at the movie screen in New York City. A demonstration of 10,000 people resulted in a riot in Boston.

However, the controversy surrounding *Birth of a Nation* only brought the film added publicity and increased ticket sales.

In this atmosphere, Simmons began his drive to revive the Klan. After finding a small group of followers in Atlanta, he held the first initiation rite on Stone Mountain. The Thanksgiving night ceremony was carefully timed by Simmons to take advantage of the opening of *Birth of a Nation* ten days later in Atlanta.

On December 6, 1915, Atlanta newspapers carried an advertisement for *Birth of a Nation*. The papers also contained the first ad for the Knights of the Ku Klux Klan, which featured the striking drawing of a hooded Klansman on horseback. Billed as "The World's

Greatest Secret, Social, Patriotic, Fraternal, Beneficiary Order," the Klan asked "Men of Intelligence and Character" to contact "Col. W. J. Simmons, Founder & Imperial Wizard."

Despite the popularity of *Birth of a Nation*, Simmons found few people willing to pay the $10 fee to join his Klan. In part, that was because Simmons designed the new Klan as a typical fraternal order. As such, he stressed the social aspects rather than the night-riding terror of the original Klan.

The appeal of the new Klan was its secret ritual, much of which seems silly today. As head of the Klan, Simmons referred to himself as "Imperial Wizard of the Invisible Empire of the Knights of the Ku-Klux Klan." Officers of local chapters included the "Exalted Cyclops" (president), "Klaliff" (vice president), "Kludd" (chaplain), "Kligrapp" (secretary), and "Klabee" (treasurer).

Klan ritual was spelled out in the Kloran, a fifty-four-page pamphlet written by Simmons, who developed and copyrighted the secret mysteries of "Klankraft." The Kloran gave instructions for the holding of "Konklaves" (meetings) by "Klaverns" (local chapters).

The bulk of the Kloran was devoted to explaining the initiation ceremony for new members. Candidates had to listen to speeches, songs, and prayers expressing the spirit and beliefs of Klanishness. Apparently to prevent any laughter, initiates were warned: "This is a serious undertaking; we are not here to make sport of you nor indulge in the silly frivolity of circus clowns."

Yet Klanishness often appeared clownish. Klansmen had their own language so that they could recognize fellow members and communicate in secret. A typical "Klonversation" in code went as follows:

"AYAK?"

"AKIA."

"CYGNAR?"

"NO. 1, ATGA."

"KIGY."

"SAN BOG."

Decoded into English, this meant:

"**Are You A K**lansman?"

"**A K**lansman **I A**m."

"**Can You Give Number And R**ealm?"

"**Number One**, Atlanta, Ga."

"**K**lansman, **I G**reet You."

"**Strangers Are Near. Be On** Guard."

The Klan also had its own Kalendar for sending secret messages. The seven days of the week were referred to as "dark, deadly, dismal, doleful, desolate, dreadful, and desperate." The weeks of the month became "woeful, weeping, wailing, wonderful, and weird," and the twelve months of the year were "bloody, gloomy, hideous, fearful, furious, alarming, terrible, horrible, mournful, sorrowful, frightful, and appalling." Dating the beginning of time from the birth of the original secret order in 1866, Klansmen could thus say that Simmons' revival of the Klan on November 25, 1915, took place on "the Doleful Day of the Wonderful Week of the Frightful Month of the Year of the Klan XLIX."

Despite the apparent foolishness of some Klankraft, the Kloran contained some serious and even frightening provisions. Membership was limited to native-born, white, Protestant American men. Klansmen took an oath pledging themselves not only to practice Klanishness but also "to maintain forever white supremacy in all things." In order to "keep Anglo-Saxon American civilizations, institutions, politics, and society pure," the Kloran called for "preventing unwarranted strikes by foreign agitators" and enacting "sensible and patriotic immigration laws." In short, "patriotic Klanishness" included attitudes that were antiblack, anti-Catholic, anti-Semitic, antilabor and anti-immigrant. Finally, the Kloran warned that violation of the Klan oath "means disgrace, dishonor, and death."

The Klan's message was clearly designed to appeal to people who were deeply troubled by a number of abrupt changes in American society. During the early years of this century, European immigrants poured into the United States at a rate of about 1 million persons a year. This tide of newcomers provided the labor that helped make America the richest country in the world. In some places American-born workers were displaced by immigrants, who worked for lower wages. But it was not job competition that created the greatest opposition to foreigners. As the number of immigrants grew, so too did the fear of them, mainly because they had customs different from those of the majority of Americans born in this country. Religious hatreds were especially aroused by the large number of Catholics and Jews that migrated to the United States. For many native-born, Protestant Americans, the new immigration represented primarily a social and cultural menace to traditional Protestant values. Explaining the threats faced by the country, Imperial Wizard Simmons once said, "The dangers were in the tremendous influx of foreign immigration, tutored in alien dogmas and alien creeds, flowing in from all climates and slowly pushing the native-born white American population into the center of the country, there to be ultimately overwhelmed and smothered."

The outbreak of World War I in 1914 slowed the wave of immigration to a trickle, but the war brought other consequences after America joined the fight against Germany in 1917. Wartime propaganda stimulated prejudice against foreigners. A government-sponsored campaign appealed for "100 per cent Americanism" in the crusade against the "Hun," as the German enemy was called. Anyone who interfered with the war effort, even workers who struck for better wages, was branded as a German agent. Meanwhile, the war presented new opportunities for black Americans who served in the armed forces or moved from the South to take jobs in northern factories. Observers began to talk about the emergence of the "new Negro," who would demand social and economic equality after the war.

For several years after its rebirth in 1915, the Ku Klux Klan grew slowly. Its initial emphasis on secret social activities made it little different from dozens of other fraternal orders. Then, the Klan was also almost wiped out by a money-hungry official who ran off with the treasury. To keep his dream alive, Simmons mortgaged his house and lived a Spartan life.

"There were times during those five early years, before the public knew of the Klan," the Imperial Wizard later recalled, "when I walked down the streets with my shoes worn through because I had no money."

World War I provided the Klan with an opportunity to show its patriotism. Hooded Klansmen in Georgia and Alabama marched in parades and hunted for draft dodgers. They also engaged in the kind of illegal actions that were all too common as a result of the wartime hysteria. When strikes threatened in several Alabama cities, they were prevented by Klansmen who kidnapped union leaders.

Such activities brought the Klan some favorable publicity and new recruits. Yet a year after World War I ended in 1918, the Klan remained a small fraternal order confined to the South. The group had fewer than 2,000 members. This hardly fulfilled Simmons' dream of an enormous national organization dedicated to Klanishness.

However, the following decade proved more receptive to Klan doctrines. With the 1920s came the heyday of the reborn Ku Klux Klan.

3 / Salesmen of Hate—
The Growth of the Klan

THE INVISIBLE EMPIRE OF THE KU KLUX KLAN FIRST BECAME NAtionally visible in the early 1920s. The fortunes of the Klan brightened considerably when its founder, Colonel Simmons, linked up with two hard-headed advertising agents, Edward Young Clarke and Elizabeth Tyler. Clarke, a young man in his thirties, was a former newspaperman from Atlanta who had tried a variety of money-making schemes but with little success. In search of new opportunities after World War I, Clarke had created the Southern Publicity Association in partnership with Tyler, a forceful, heavy-set woman with a head for business. After some success organizing fund-raising campaigns for groups like the Red Cross and the Anti-Saloon League, Clarke and Tyler decided the Ku Klux Klan could make them rich.

"We came into contact with Colonel Simmons and the Ku Klux Klan through the fact that my son-in-law joined it," Mrs. Tyler later recalled. "We found Colonel Simmons was having a hard time to get along. He couldn't pay his rent. His receipts were not sufficient to take care of his personal needs. . . . After we had investigated it from every angle, we decided to go into it with Colonel Simmons and give it the impetus that it could get best from publicity."

In June, 1920, Clarke and Simmons signed a contract that guaranteed Clarke a share of Klan profits. The agreement made Clarke Imperial Kleagle of the Knights of the Ku Klux

Klan and put him in charge of recruiting. In return for securing new members, Clarke was to receive 80 percent of every Klectoken (initiation fee) of $10. The remaining 20 percent went to Imperial Wizard Simmons. Clarke had to pay his own expenses, but he quickly showed that kluxing (recruiting) could turn big profits.

Clarke and his business partner, Tyler, soon flooded the country with a sales force of Kleagles that sold Klan memberships on a commission basis. Out of every $10 klectoken, $4 went to the Kleagle, $1 to the King Kleagle (state organizer), 50 cents to the Grand Goblin (regional director), and $2.50 to Clarke and Tyler. The final share of $2 went to Colonel Simmons. Driven by this financial incentive, the salesmen of hate appealed to local fears and anxieties to bring white, native-born, Protestant men into the secret order, which was presented as a defender of "100 per cent Americanism."

In little more than a year, an effective promotional campaign brought over 85,000 new members into the Invisible Empire. With them came $850,000 in initiation fees, which were divided among Klan organizers. Clarke and Tyler received $212,000. Part of this went to purchase an old mansion in Atlanta that became Klan headquarters—"the Imperial Palace." Colonel Simmons' share amounted to $170,000, and he also received $25,000 in back pay and a comfortable home in Atlanta, which he named "Klankrest."

The colonel's dream of a national organization of hooded Klansmen was fast becoming a reality under the practical leadership of Clarke and Tyler. "They made things hum all over America," Simmons once declared.

The Klan's spectacular growth increased the visibility of the Invisible Empire. A New York newspaper, *The World*, first exposed the activities of the Klan in a series of articles that was reprinted in cities across the country. The exposé included evidence that Klansmen had engaged in violence, particularly in the South. Following this disclosure, a congressional committee investigated the Klan. At public hearings in Washington during October, 1921, Colonel Simmons passionately defended his group against charges that its secrecy concealed acts of terror against Catholics, Jews, and blacks. The Invisible Empire, according to Simmons, would not tolerate any lawless deeds by its members. "Our mask and robe, I say before God, are as innocent as the breath of an angel," the Imperial Wizard told congressmen.

These early attempts to expose the Klan backfired. Newspaper descriptions of Klan ritual and violence attracted new members, some of whom used sample application forms that illustrated the newspaper articles. A week of inconclusive congressional hearings simply gave the Imperial Wizard a national platform.

"It wasn't until the newspapers began to attack the Klan that it really grew," Colonel Simmons later recalled. "Certain newspapers also aided us by inducing Congress to investigate us. The result was that Congress gave us the best advertising we got. Congress made us." Membership in the Klan reportedly expanded at the rate of 5,000 a day after Simmons had testified in Washington.

However, the popularity of the Ku Klux Klan was due to more than publicity and good salesmanship. The resurgence of the Klan in the early 1920s came at a time when many Americans felt threatened by a variety of recent changes. The 1920 census reported that for the first time in history the majority of Americans were living in cities. Although this condition was the result of long-term shifts in population, it also represented a cultural challenge to native-born, Protestant, rural Americans who were worried about the city becoming an alien force dominated by Catholic and Jewish immigrants and their children. World War I had temporarily stopped the flow of Europeans to the United States, but after the war ended in 1918 immigration resumed, with almost 1 million foreigners arriving in 1920-21. The mounting opposition to further immigration was also fed by an economic depression that hit the United States in the early 1920s.

At the same time, the nation was beset by a crime wave. The adoption of Prohibition in 1920 made it illegal for Americans to manufacture or sell any alcoholic beverage. Since many people still wanted such drinks, bootleggers, moonshiners, and rumrunners illegally supplied beer and liquor. The violation of Prohibition led, in the view of its supporters, to other vices, such as gambling and prostitution.

By 1920, many Americans thought their country was coming apart at the seams. In this climate, the Ku Klux Klan presented itself as a defender of "100 per cent Americanism." This vague slogan proved popular because it could mean almost anything to the frightened men who flocked into the Invisible Empire.

The white, native-born Protestants who joined the Klan were undoubtedly driven by a variety of motives. For some, the Klan stood as a barrier against so-called "foreign" influences, particularly Roman Catholicism. Overlooking constitutional guarantees of religious freedom, the Klan took the position that "America is Protestant and so it must remain." The burning cross became a symbol of this commitment.

Other Klansmen hoped the Invisible Empire would keep blacks "in their place." As one Klan leader put it, "Every instinct, every interest, every dictate of conscience and public spirit, insist that white supremacy shall be forever maintained."

The cry for "100 per cent Americanism" could also be used to uphold traditional morality, especially when threatened by bootleggers and other law breakers. Parading Klansmen often carried signs that proclaimed, LAW AND ORDER MUST PREVAIL.

The broad appeal of the Klan was best summarized in a handout used for recruiting:

> Every criminal, every gambler, every thug, every libertine, every girl ruiner, every home wrecker, every wife beater, every dope peddler, every moonshiner, every crooked politician, every pagan Papist priest, every shyster lawyer, every white slaver, every brothel madam, every Rome controlled newspaper, every black spider—is fighting the Klan. Think it over. Which side are you on?

Taking advantage of the fears of troubled Americans, the Klan's salesmen enrolled over 1 million members by the end of 1922.

Kluxing paid off for Klan officials. In addition to the money from initiation fees and annual dues, cash poured in for the purchase of white robes and hoods that became the uniform of the well-dressed Klansman. "We charged $6.50 for costumes and were making $1 on each sale," Colonel Simmons declared. As a result of these money-making schemes, the Imperial Wizard estimated that Americans gave the Klan over $12 million a year at its peak. "Look at the money some of the organizers and field men made," Simmons reflected almost in disbelief. As an example, the Grand Goblin of the Domain of the Southwest, a regional director with headquarters in Houston, admitted that his monthly income was about $4,000, and there were others like him around the country. One disillusioned Kleagle concluded that the Klan was "clearly a money-making scheme run for the benefit of a few insiders."

However, the founder of the Klan saw little of the money. Colonel Simmons had the satisfaction of seeing his dream of a national order of hooded Klansmen become a reality, but most of the profits went to others. Even worse for him, his personal triumph lasted only a short time.

The hard-headed salesmen of hate who built the Klan quickly turned Simmons' dream into a nightmare. First, it was revealed that Imperial Kleagle Clarke and Mrs. Tyler were scarcely models of virtue. The two had been arrested for disorderly conduct shortly before becoming Klan organizers. When newspapers published this story, Tyler quietly retired in 1922, claiming poor health. Clarke continued as Imperial Kleagle, but his reputation was further damaged by his arrest in Indiana for possessing liquor just after he had delivered a speech calling for better enforcement of Prohibition. Some Klansmen also charged that Clarke mishandled Klan funds. When Colonel Simmons failed to take any action against Clarke, other Klansmen seized control of the Invisible Empire.

The setting for the takeover was the first national Klonvocation (convention) of the Klan in Atlanta late in 1922. Imperial Wizard Simmons called the meeting in hopes that the 1,000 delegates would reaffirm his leadership. Several Grand Dragons (state leaders) had other ideas. They used the occasion to trick the trusting Simmons into accepting the exalted title of Emperor while the real power passed to a new Imperial Wizard. Simmons agreed to the change after he was told that any attempt to retain the post of Imperial Wizard would result in dishonor and bloodshed. The conspirators awakened Simmons in the middle of the night before the Klonvocation and pretended to come to his defense.

According to Simmons, he was told: "There is a certain crowd of men who say if you are nominated for the office of Imperial Wizard tomorrow, they will get up on the floor and attack your character. And we've just come to tell you that the first man who insults your name will be killed by a sharpshooter right on the spot as he speaks. There'll be enough of us with firearms to take care of the whole convention, if necessary."

Fooled by this story, Simmons agreed to become Emperor and let someone else take over as Imperial Wizard. He also accepted the suggestion that this man be Dr. Hiram Wesley Evans, and the following day the Klonvocation formally ratified the decisions. "I didn't know at first that my interests had been harmed in any way," Colonel Simmons later recalled. "I had complete confidence in all these men."

Even an impractical dreamer like Simmons could quickly discover that he had lost control of the Invisible Empire. When he went to headquarters at the Imperial Palace, he found Evans sitting at his desk.

"He didn't get up to give me my place," Simmons remembered. Instead Evans promised to build a white throne for the Emperor, but he never got around to it. "I didn't have any place to go," Simmons said sadly. "I just had to sort of hang around the place even though my title was Emperor."

The new Klan constitution adopted by the Klonvocation confirmed Simmons' worst suspicions. "I looked at the paragraph covering the powers and duties of the Emperor. I saw that every power had been taken away from me and given to the Imperial Wizard. Evans and the rest of them laughed at me, when I went to 'The Palace' to complain."

The new power in the Invisible Empire was a round-faced, pudgy dentist from Dallas, Texas. Like Simmons, Dr. Evans had belonged to a number of fraternal orders before joining the Klan. Evans, however, had the leadership qualities to rise from Exalted Cyclops (chapter president) of the Dallas Klavern and become Imperial Wizard of the entire Klan. Evans reportedly combined "the determined convictions of Martin Luther, the kindness of Lincoln, and the strategy and generalship of Napoleon." After unseating Simmons, Evans solidified his position by cancelling Edward Clarke's contract, which had given him control over 80 percent of the initiation fees. Evans had thus become chief executive officer and chief salesman for the Klan.

The inept Colonel Simmons tried to recapture his former power and prestige, but he was no match for Evans. When he sought to tell his side of the story, his enemies outsmarted him.

"I tried to tell Klansmen what had happened to the Klan, but I couldn't get a hearing," Simmons complained. "Klansmen questioned my morals. They got an old man to sit on the platform before 30,000 people in Ohio and play drunk. Secretly they told the people that the old man was Simmons. I wrote a book for Klansmen, trying to get the truth to them, but Evans issued an order banishing anyone who read it. All this time, remember, I was still the Emperor."

Simmons also tried to organize a women's branch of the Ku Klux Klan, but Evans effectively blocked this move. In addition to forbidding Klansmen from cooperating with Simmons, Evans formed a competing women's auxiliary, Women of the Ku Klux Klan. With a woman as Imperial Commander, the group quickly claimed some 250,000 members, most of them related to Klansmen. Wearing the familiar white hoods and robes, Klanswomen joined Klansmen in torchlight rallies and cross burnings. Above all, Klanswomen added to the power of Evans and his Invisible Empire.

The growing feud between Evans and Simmons wound up before the courts and on the front page of newspapers. Legal charges and countercharges led to an out-of-court settlement that guaranteed Simmons $1,000 a month for the rest of his life in return for his copyrights to the Klan's ritual and regalia. Despite this agreement, the feuding continued, with each side attacking the other publicly. The conflict even drew blood when Phillip Fox, a supporter of Evans, murdered William S. Coburn, Simmons' attorney. (Fox was tried, found guilty, and sentenced to life imprisonment.)

Finally, Evans banished Simmons from the Invisible Empire and paid him off with a lump sum of $146,000 in 1924. Simmons' retirement left Evans as undisputed head of the Ku Klux Klan, and he remained in that position until 1939.

While Imperial leaders in Atlanta fought over the spoils, the Klan spread across the country during the early 1920s. Led by Imperial Kleagle Edward Clarke, recruiters moved into southern states, where they signed up thousands of Klansmen, some of whom resorted to violence to enforce their views. Despite disclaimers by Imperial Wizard Simmons, the reign of terror in the South continued until Simmons was deposed by Evans in 1923. Meanwhile, recruiters moved outside the South to the Midwest and Far West, where the Klan found its greatest following. There violence was rarely used by Klansmen. By 1923 the Klan had become a national force, but it employed different tactics in different regions.

4/Hooded Night Riders—
The Klan in the South

DURING THE EARLY 1920s, THE KU KLUX KLAN FREQUENTLY TRAVELED on a wave of terror in the South and Southwest. Indeed, the Invisible Empire sometimes used terror to announce its presence and spur recruitment. As Klan violence spread a pattern emerged. The victims were generally white, native-born Protestants who had broken some local moral code. Bootleggers and gamblers were favorite targets. In addition, the Klan went to the defense of the family by attacking people suspected of adultery, wife beating, or child neglect.

Taking the law into their own hands, hooded Klansmen sometimes seized their victims in broad daylight, but more often they piled into cars after dark and went "night-riding," as their marauding became known. The tools of their illegal trade were whips, buckets of tar, and bags of pillow feathers. After stripping the clothing from a person, these masked defenders of American morals would apply enough lashes of the whip to tear the skin and leave permanent scars. They then poured tar on the victim and sprinkled feathers on the sticky coating to add insult to injury. In the worst cases, Klan sadism could lead to mutilation and even death.

The Invisible Empire also used thinly veiled threats of violence to enforce its view of morality. Klansmen in full regalia silently paraded through towns at night. Often the town's streetlights mysteriously went dark with the help of cooperative local officials. The hooded marchers, some on horseback, carried their message on banners. In the eerie light of flaming torches, bystanders could read slogans declaring "Booze Must Go," "Crap Shooters Beware," "Pure Womanhood," "The Guilty Must Pay." The calling card of the Invisible Empire became the burning cross ignited in the front yard of someone who could clearly expect much worse if he did not mend his ways.

In Mobile, Alabama, Klansmen left little doubt that they would back up their threats with force. A public notice issued by the Klan in the early 1920s read:

> Law violators! This is the first and last time that we will warn you! You must either heed this warning or take the consequences. . . . This warning is for the taxi drivers, street smashers, bad women, shinny dealers, gamblers, thieves, loafers, and any and all violators of the law. Should you violate one of the laws after receiving this warning, be ye assured that we will attend to you without hesitation.

Despite all the evidence to the contrary, Klan leaders routinely denied that the Knights of the Invisible Empire committed acts of violence. Testifying before Congress in 1921, Imperial Wizard Simmons had declared: "The Klan does not countenance nor will it tolerate any lawless acts by its members. Instead we teach respect for the law." Simmons emphasized that "whenever a man presumes to take the law into his own hands and to commit a misdeed against his fellow citizens, that man, under our regulations, is automatically out of this organization."

The official defense of the Klan overlooked the fact that the secret group was modeled after the Reconstruction Klan, which had been an instrument of terror. Furthermore, the new Klan, like the old, was designed to hide the identity of Klansmen. The uniform achieved this purpose by cloaking members in a long white robe and a peaked white hood that included a full face mask with only eye holes cut in it. Night-riding Klansmen were concealed not only from their victims but also from each other, which undoubtedly increased the temptation to resort to lawlessness.

A Texas judge publicly described a Klansman as someone who "picks up a newspaper and sees where there has been a miscarriage of justice, then broods over this iniquity, turns one hundred per cent American, sends $16.50 to Georgia, buckles on a pistol, covers his face with a mask, dresses in a long, white robe, leaves his family, and goes out into the darkness and disturbs another man's family by trying to stop crime waves with a bucket of tar and feathers."

By taking the law into their own hands, Klansmen became nothing more than vigilantes. The tradition of vigilante justice had deep roots in nineteenth century America, when it was commonly used to deal with horse thieves, cattle rustlers, and other outlaws. On the American frontier, private citizens often acted as sheriff, judge, and jury because regular law enforcement had not yet been established or was too weak to be effective. Although illegal, vigilante methods proved so effective that they continued to be used long after frontier conditions had disappeared. As the setting for vigilante violence shifted from the countryside to cities, so too did the nature of the victims change. By the early 1920s, the targets included not simply common criminals but also Catholics, Jews, blacks, political radicals, union organizers, and anyone else considered "undesirable" in a local community. Such people had usually committed no crime, which is why in most cases a mob of vigilantes, rather than police, went after them. Despite changes in vigilantism, it remained essentially a violent, illegal means of trying to make people conform to some local standard of conduct.

This illegal method of regulating society proved especially popular in the South and Southwest during the 1920s. The punishment was swift and cheap. Also, as one defender of the Klan pointed out, "the advantage of the protection afforded by the K.K.K. is that it can rid the community of undesirables *before* they commit some serious offense."

Although Klansmen engaged in illegal activities, they rarely ran into trouble with the law. Night riders were shielded not only by their hoods but also by public officials, including policemen, who were often fellow Klansmen. The high level of Klan violence in Dallas was in part due to the fact that the head of the police force was a prominent member of the Invisible Empire. According to historian Charles C. Alexander, "Practically every city in the Southwest came under the dominance of the Klan." Leaders of the Invisible Empire used the general lack of indictments against Klansmen as proof that the Klan did not break the law. However, the official Klan newspaper declared in 1921, "it doubtless is amusing to members of the Knights of the Ku-Klux Klan to hear a judge

33

instruct a grand jury to probe that organization because of its 'lawlessness and un-Americanism,' when they know that anywhere from a third to one-half the members of the grand jury are members of the K.K.K."

Even though few individual Klansmen were found guilty of violating the law during the 1920s, the Klan systematically used terror in some areas. The worst mob violence occurred in Texas, Oklahoma, Louisiana, and Arkansas. In rapidly growing cities like Dallas, Tulsa, and Shreveport, a morally aroused public worried about evil forces. Klan recruiters who spread through the Southwest appealed to local fears and signed up over 200,000 members by 1922. Drawing on a strong local tradition of vigilantism, the Klan's drive for "law and order" soon turned into a reign of terror in the region. The victims, most of them white, included suspected bootleggers, gamblers, adulterers, and other "sinners" who were kidnapped, whipped, and tarred and feathered by hooded night riders.

Texas provided some of the worst examples of mob violence. Hooded Klansmen first appeared in Houston in 1920 when they kidnapped and tarred and feathered a lawyer for having too many black clients. In Dallas, a black bellhop was dragged from his job by masked men who forced him into a waiting car. Accused of associating with white women, the young man was flogged with a whip, and the letters "K.K.K." were burned on his forehead with acid. In 1922 some sixty people fell victim to beatings in the Dallas area. In another Texas town, hooded men in white robes beat and tarred and feathered a woman charged with bigamy. A doctor suspected of performing abortions was flogged by Klansmen who later bragged of their feat in a letter to the local newspaper.

In 1921, a Houston newspaper concluded that "Texas Klansmen have beaten and blackened more people in the last six months than [Klansmen from] all the other states combined." Despite the countless acts of mob violence, only one resulted in any punishment of Klan members. Twelve admitted members of Goose Creek Klan No. 8 were fined $100 each for beating a man and woman near Houston. Even in this case, a Klan newspaper bragged about the results. "It cost the boys down there $1200 to transform a rough and tumble oil camp into a progressive and God-fearing community of industrious toilers. . . . The Ku Klux Klan has made a new and different town of Goose Creek."

34

Oklahoma's record of Klan violence probably surpassed that of any other state. In 1923, the state's governor, Jack Walton, declared martial law to stem the tide of violence. An inquiry by the National Guard discovered evidence of dozens of floggings in Tulsa County alone. A military court sentenced four confessed Klan floggers to prison, but only one ever served any time. Governor Walton had stepped on too many toes, and he found himself impeached and removed from office by the state legislature. His successor as governor pardoned the only Klansman in jail and dismissed the charges against the others accused of participating in flogging parties.

The most infamous example of Klan violence occurred in northern Louisiana. There the Klan's arrival intensified a long-standing rivalry between the towns of Mer Rouge and Bastrop, both located in Morehouse Parish (county). The residents of Mer Rouge, a small village built on cotton plantations, rarely saw eye to eye with the citizens of Bastrop, an industrial town that also served as the parish seat. In 1921, Bastrop embraced the Klan wholeheartedly. Prominent members included the mayor, the sheriff, the prosecuting attorney, and the postmaster. The Exalted Cyclops of the Bastrop Klavern was Captain J. K. Skipwith, a Confederate veteran, member of the original Klan, and former mayor of Bastrop. The aging Skipwith and some 200 fellow Klansmen set out to clean up Morehouse Parish, especially Mer Rouge, which quickly became a center of opposition to the Invisible Empire. However, the Klan's attacks on bootleggers were popular in Bastrop. According to the local newspaper, "It may be a dangerous remedy to apply—this Ku Klux business—but sometimes bad diseases require heroic treatment."

The cure proved worse than the disease as the level of violence in the parish rose. During August, 1922, masked men wearing black Klan robes blocked a procession of Mer Rouge residents returning home after a parish picnic and baseball game. At gunpoint, the night riders seized F. Watt Daniel, Thomas F. Richards, Daniel's father, and two other men. The last three were released after receiving beatings, but Watt Daniel and Thomas Richards were never seen alive again. Both men had been previously threatened by the Klan because of their outspoken criticism of the Invisible Empire.

After a Morehouse Parish grand jury—dominated by local Klansmen—failed to take any action in the case of the missing men, Richards' wife appealed to the governor of Louisiana for help. Troubled by the spread of Klan terror, Governor John M. Parker declared war on the Invisible Empire. "Neither mob violence nor the Ku Klux Klan shall run this state," he announced. "The law must and shall prevail."

In order to solve the case of the missing men, Governor Parker took the unusual step of asking for federal assistance. His request brought a team of federal agents to investigate. However, many Louisiana politicians claimed the disappearance was not a federal issue, and the resulting furor focused national attention on the Mer Rouge case.

Federal agents concluded that Daniel and Richards were probably dead and at the bottom of one of the many lakes in the Parish. When Governor Parker called out the National Guard to search for the bodies, a mysterious dynamite explosion rocked Lake Lafourche. Apparently designed to destroy evidence, the charge brought two badly mangled bodies to the surface. From pieces of clothing, authorities identified the corpses as the two men who had disappeared after being kidnapped four months earlier.

Americans expressed outrage at the crime. A New Orleans paper called it "one of the foulest crimes that has ever stained the annals of Louisiana." Most people blamed the Klan for the killings. "The Ku Klux Klan as an organization will repudiate the crime," observed a New Jersey newspaper. "But in the wider court of public opinion the wizards and the cyclopses and dragons will have to present a convincing case before the American people will cease to believe that Daniel and Richards were killed because they refused to bow before the authority of an organization having no standing in law or morals."

Klan leaders claimed that no murder had been committed and that the bodies were planted in the lake by detectives. According to a Klan newspaper, the bodies "were shipped in there and placed in the lake either to force a confession from the Klan or to fan the flames of public prejudice against the Order."

Morehouse Parish grand juries, containing known Klansmen, failed to charge anyone with the murders. Despite evidence that Klansmen had abducted Daniel and Richards, two grand juries concluded that there was insufficient evidence to bring anyone to trial.

The Imperial Wizard of the Klan called this a complete vindication of the Invisible Empire, but the publicity surrounding the case severely hurt the Klan's image as a defender of law and order.

Indeed, the Klan's reputation for mob violence had become a cause for concern among national leaders of the organization. In 1923, Imperial Wizard Hiram Wesley Evans, who had usurped Simmons' position as head of the Klan, spoke out against violence in an attempt to save the Klan from itself. "Violent methods are never justifiable," he declared, "not even when the ordinary agencies of law have broken down. Violent measures should never be used."

Some lessening of violence did occur, and by 1924 the Klan's reign of illegal terror had largely come to an end in the South. Meanwhile, the Invisible Empire had crossed the Mason-Dixon line in the early 1920s, and it had captured a large following in the Midwest and Far West. With a growing, well-organized power base, the Klan moved increasingly into the legal arena of politics, where it achieved its most notable victories during the decade of the twenties.

5 / Ku Klux Kandidates

ON DECEMBER 22, 1921, 6,000 PEOPLE FLOCKED TO THE FIRST PUBLIC rally of the Ku Klux Klan in Portland, Oregon. A local Protestant minister told his sympathetic audience that the Klan had come to Portland, "not simply for a brief visit, but to be enrolled among the permanent organizations of your city." Within six months, Portland's Klan No. 1 had over 10,000 members.

The Invisible Empire spread through Portland the same way it would in many other cities outside the South. The campaign began secretly when a Kleagle (recruiter), Luther I. Powell, went to Portland in the summer of 1921. Avoiding publicity, Powell quietly sold the Klan's version of "100 per cent Americanism" to interested members of local fraternal and civic groups. Within a few months, the Kleagle had signed up enough Knights to hold the first official initiation. In December, 1921, the Portland Klan felt strong enough to call its first public rally, which drew an overflow crowd to the 5,000-seat city auditorium.

Henceforth, the carefully orchestrated recruiting campaign operated openly with enormous success. Monster Klan rallies brought protests from Catholic groups, who objected to the use of the city-owned auditorium, but Portland's mayor—reputed to be a Klansman himself—refused to move against the hooded order.

Meanwhile, the Portland Klan took a number of steps designed to win public approval and additional recruits. The Invisible Empire pledged $50,000 to a children's home and held a Christmas party featuring Kris Kringle. The group also organized a "Klan Kommunity Kit" to compete with the Community Chest, which supported Catholic and Jewish charities. The Klan's commitment to Protestantism was publicized by church visits that became a kind of ritual. Typically, a small group of Klansmen would interrupt a Sunday service without any prior warning. Hidden by hoods and robes, the Knights dramatically marched down the aisle, handed the minister an offering of money, and then silently departed. On occasion, a Klansman or the minister himself would explain the purpose of the secret order and invite churchgoers to join. Constant reminders of the Klan's presence in Portland also included noisy automobile Kavelkades and cross burnings on nearby mountains.

Although strongest in Portland, the Invisible Empire spread to other Oregon cities, including Salem and Eugene. By the spring of 1922, the Klan had an estimated 14,000 members in the northwestern state. Over 10,000 of them were in Portland, which became state headquarters for one of the most powerful Klan organizations in the country.

On the surface, Oregon seemed an unlikely state to attract the Klan. Almost 90 percent of its residents were native-born, over 90 percent were Protestant, and virtually all were white. However, prejudice was not related to numbers, and the state proved to be exceedingly anti-Catholic. The Klan exploited this hatred by hurling a barrage of its usual anti-Catholic propaganda. One lecturer gave Oregon audiences a taste of how far the Klan would go to prevent a Catholic from becoming president of the United States. "As one American I stand before you to contend that we have enough real red-blooded Protestant American citizens to swear with our hand raised to heaven that we will float our horses in blood to their bridles before we will see a Roman Catholic sitting in our presidential chair." The Exalted Cyclops of Portland once remarked that "the only way to cure a Catholic is to kill him."

The Oregon Klan used its well-organized membership and its anti-Catholic appeal to capture control of the state government in 1922. The Klan's political target was Governor Ben Olcott, who had dared to speak out against the group. The Klan retaliated by endorsing one of Olcott's opponents in the Republican primary election during the spring of 1922. Warning of the Klan's growing power, Olcott told voters just before the election: "Dangerous forces are insidiously gaining a foothold in Oregon. In the guise of a secret society, parading under the name of the Ku Klux Klan, these forces are endeavoring to usurp the reign of government, are stirring up fanaticism, race hatred, religious prejudice, and all of those evil influences which tend toward factional strife and civil terror." Having made the Klan the number one issue in the primary campaign, Governor Olcott barely won renomination by a 500-vote margin.

The general election in November, 1922, gave the Invisible Empire another chance to defeat Governor Olcott. However, Klansmen faced seemingly impossible odds, since Olcott had the Republican nomination and Republicans outnumbered Democrats by more than two to one in Oregon. Nevertheless, the Klan endorsed Walter Pierce, the Democratic candidate for governor, who openly supported the proposal that all children, including those then in Catholic schools, be required to attend public schools.

The Klan's anti-Catholic campaign helped make Walter Pierce Oregon's first Democratic governor in half a century. In a decisive electoral victory, Pierce defeated Governor Olcott by a vote of 132,000 to 98,000.

Although it probably had less than 15,000 members in Oregon, the Klan showed that a well-organized campaign could successfully appeal to a great reservoir of anti-Catholic prejudice. Many voters who did not actually join the group would support its opposition to Catholics and other minorities. The Klan's resulting political power enabled it to capture control of Oregon's state legislature in the 1922 election. The Speaker of the House became K. K. Kubli, a long-time legislator whose initials had won him a free membership in the secret fraternity.

Since the Klan's program was largely negative, it found few positive ways to use its political power. However, in Oregon it achieved its earliest and greatest political victory with the proposed abolition of parochial schools. A law passed in 1922 required that after 1926 all children in the state had to attend public schools whether they wanted to or not. (In 1925, the United States Supreme Court ruled the Oregon law unconstitutional.)

Reflecting on the Klan's sudden rise to power in Oregon, Governor Olcott once remarked: "We woke up one morning and found the Klan had about gained political control of the state. Practically not a word had been raised against them." Other northern and western states were subject to the same kind of campaign, which put Ku Klux Kandidates in local and state offices.

In the early 1920s, when Klan Kleagles fanned out across the United States to recruit new members, Imperial Wizard Simmons was asked if only Southerners could join the Invisible Empire. He replied, "Any real man, any native-born white American citizen who is not affiliated with any foreign institution and who loves his country and his flag may become a member of the Ku Klux Klan, whether he lives north, south, east or west." From Maine to California, Kleagles found thousands of people willing to pay $10 to fight for "100 per cent Americanism." The exact size of the Klan will never be known, since membership lists were a closely guarded secret, but anywhere from 2 million to 4 million Americans flocked into the Invisible Empire during the 1920s. That made it the largest fraternal order in the country and a highly visible political force.

Spurred on by the financial rewards promised by Edward Clarke and Elizabeth Tyler, Kleagles used a variety of methods to recruit members, but a similar pattern emerged, especially in the North and West, where Klansmen rarely resorted to violence. Like other door-to-door salesmen, Klan organizers first approached prominent citizens of a community and appealed to a variety of motives for joining the Klan. The Invisible Empire not only held up lofty ideals like "100 per cent Americanism," but it also promised specific benefits for members. Businessmen could display the coded message "TWK," meaning "Trade with Klansmen," which would presumably increase profits as the Klan grew. Politicians could dream of enlarging their power by linking up with the KKK. Protestant ministers quickly found that the Klan's emphasis on religion helped swell church attendance.

After signing up a few well-known citizens, Kleagles turned their attention to the rest of the community. According to one observer, "hustling agents sought out the poor, the romantic, the short-witted, the bored, the vindictive, the bigoted, and the ambitious, and sold them their heart's desire." The Klan could be all things to all men—if they happened to be native-born white Protestants looking for scapegoats to blame their problems on. Sometimes newspaper ads were used to publicize Klan movies or lecturers, brought in to aid recruiting drives. The high point of the campaign was often an outdoor rally where Klansmen were initiated into the hooded order by the light of torches and burning crosses.

The Klan had originally billed itself as "A Classy Order of the Highest Class," but it showed little concern with screening applicants. Anyone willing to pay the Klectoken could join. One former organizer declared that "Kleagles were selling memberships as they would sell insurance or stock." A sympathetic study of the Klan could not find "a single case where a Kleagle refused a member—who had $10.00—no matter how vicious or dangerous he might be." Yet most Klansmen were probably law-abiding, churchgoing family men, though fearful and narrow-minded in their views. A cross section of conservative Protestants, from prosperous businessmen to blue-collar factory workers, joined the Invisible Empire. One prominent Klansman was Gutzon Borglum, the sculptor who carved the likenesses of four Presidents on Mount Rushmore. Most Klansmen were middle-class and lower-middle-class Americans who never engaged in any violence. They had in common their fear of rapid social changes in America and their assumption that "evil" influences—Catholics, Jews, blacks, alcohol—were responsible for the country's problems.

Despite outrageous incidents of Klan-inspired violence in the South, the Klan generally used the vote, rather than the whip, to attack its sworn enemies. The Invisible Empire became most visible by entering the political arena in order to defend "100 per cent Americanism." For Klansmen, that meant using their power to check the political influence of so-called "un-American" groups like Catholics, Jews, and recent immigrants. Catholics were the greatest concern in the mind of newly elected Imperial Wizard Evans, who announced in 1923 that "we shall steadfastly oppose the political interference of Roman Catholic organizations in political matters in America." According to the Klan, Catholic groups were supposedly controlled by the church hierarchy led by the Pope in Rome.

Klansmen also hoped to eliminate vice and corruption through the ballot box. Summarizing the Klan attitude, one Knight declared: "Everybody knows that politicians nowadays cater to all kinds of 'elements,' mostly selfish, some corrupt, and some definitely anti-American. They cater to the bootleg vote, the vice vote, and sometimes even the violently criminal vote. What the Klan intends to do is make them pay some attention to the decent God-fearing, law-abiding vote." Through appeals like this the Klan commanded a large voting bloc—it gained the political support not only of members but also of many other people who shared its prejudices.

Throughout the country the Klan used a variety of political tactics with surprising effectiveness. At first, it simply tried to inform voters about the issues. That usually meant publicizing a candidate's religion and his attitude toward the Klan's version of Americanism. For example, in a state election in Wisconsin Klansmen circulated the following handout.

Below is information of a political nature. The names of the men who have a star before their names are worthy of the support of all true Americans at this particular time.

Governor Blaine	Anti-Klan, Anti-American
Lt. Governor Huber	Anti-Klan
*Secretary of State Zimmerman	
Treasurer Levitan	No information other than a Jew
*County Clerk Johnson	

If you are a hundred per cent American show it by going to the polls and casting your vote.

As the Ku Klux Klan grew in numbers, it moved directly into politics. It did not form a separate political party, but instead used its influence to swing elections by supporting or opposing particular candidates whether they happened to be Republicans or Democrats. "The Klan will educate and influence the public to vote for the best candidates in every election, regardless of party," one spokesman explained.

Because they did not form a party, Imperial leaders routinely claimed that the Invisible Empire was not involved in politics. "The Klan is not in politics, neither is it a political party," the Imperial Wizard declared in 1924 when the Klan was at the peak of its political power. But he continued, "We will permit no political party and no group of politicians to annex, own, disown, or disavow us. Where our conscience leads us, we will be found, regardless of who we find in the different political camps." Indeed, in some cases Klansmen ran openly for office, as Republicans or Democrats, with the Klan's official endorsement.

However, the Invisible Empire did not need to elect members to be effective. Power-hungry politicians bowed to the will of the Klan, since it controlled the life-blood of politics—votes. As one Klan official told a reporter: "You talk about the Klan terrifying folks. We don't aim to, except one bunch—the politicians. . . . They're scared senseless right now, big ones as well as little ones. They don't know which end they're standing on, and they duck every time any one says 'Klan.' They're scared, terrified, paralyzed, buffaloed, licked!"

The Invisible Empire won its first political victories in major southern cities during the years some Klansmen were engaged in mob violence. In 1922, it captured control of Atlanta, birthplace and headquarters of the society. Running successfully for the Atlanta City Council, the editor of the Klan newspaper, *Searchlight*, bragged, "I am the original Ku Klux Klansman, and I am proud of it. I belong to everything anti-Catholic I know of." That same year, Little Rock Klan No. 1, with over 7,000 members, elected every local candidate it supported. As a result, the Invisible Empire ran the capital city of Arkansas for several years. In Dallas, "the word of the Klan officials is law," one observer noted in the early 1920s; Klan-supported candidates held virtually every important elective office in the city. The hooded order also temporarily controlled the Texas cities of Houston, Fort Worth, and Wichita Falls.

The Klan had greater difficulty winning statewide contests, but nevertheless it helped elect two major officials in Georgia and Texas. In 1922, the Klan targeted Georgia's governor, Thomas W. Hardwick, for defeat because he had demanded that Klansmen take off their masks and reveal their membership lists. The wrath of the KKK helped defeat Hardwick and elect his opponent, Clifford Walker, who promised Klansmen, "I am not going to denounce anybody." After his election, Governor Walker admitted that he himself was a Klansman.

The biggest southern victory came in Texas, where a Klansman, Earle B. Mayfield, was elected to the U.S. Senate. When three members of the Invisible Empire announced for the office in 1922, the secret order held its own "elimination primary" to let Klansmen decide which Knight to support. With 100,000 well-organized Klansmen in the state, Mayfield won the Klan "primary," the Democratic primary, and the general election. Mayfield's opponents tried to block him from taking his seat in Washington, but the U.S. Senate refused to let Klan membership stand in the way of Mayfield's representing Texas.

The power of the Invisible Empire proved irresistible to many southern politicians, especially those just starting their careers. Among the upcoming politicians who joined the Klan was Alabama's Hugo L. Black. As a Birmingham lawyer with an eye on politics, young Black joined virtually every imaginable fraternal order, including the American Legion, Masons, Odd Fellows, Moose, Civitans, Pretorians, and Knights of Pythias. In 1923, Black secretly joined the Invisible Empire of the Knights of the Ku Klux Klan. Despite the Klan association with mob violence in Alabama, almost half the registered voters in Black's area of Jefferson County were rumored to be members. Although apparently never very active in the Klan, Black took the precaution of officially resigning in 1925 in preparation for his campaign for the U.S. Senate. This left Black in a strong position, since he could deny being a Klansman, but could presumably pick up Klan votes. Described by a Montgomery newspaper as "the darling of the Klan," the forty-year-old Black won Alabama's 1926 Senate race. In the same election, the state also chose an Exalted Cyclops, Bibb Graves, as governor.

At a statewide Klan Klorero (convention), Alabama's Grand Dragon introduced the two victors as "the men who have been chosen by the Klansmen of Alabama to come out into the forefront." The Grand Dragon then presented Black with a "Grand Passport" that declared: "The bearer Kl. Senator Hugo L. Black is a citizen of the Invisible Empire." In response Black told the audience of Klansmen: "I do not feel that it would be out of place to state to you here on this occasion that I know that without the support of the members of this organization I would not have been called, even by my enemies, the 'Junior Senator from Alabama.' "

These private statements came back to haunt Black a decade later. A few weeks after

45

fellow senators approved his nomination to the U.S. Supreme Court in 1937, a newspaperman revealed evidence of Black's old ties to the Invisible Empire. In addition to proof of his Klan membership, the reporter published a transcript of Black's indiscreet speech to the Alabama Klorero. The story, carried by papers across the country, argued that the Grand Passport accepted by Black in 1926 made the Supreme Court Justice a lifetime "member of the hooded brotherhood that for ten long, blood-drenched years ruled the Southland with lash and noose and torch."

Vacationing in Europe at the time, Justice Black returned home to deal with the charges. In a nationwide radio address, Black frankly admitted, "I did join the Klan." However, he added that he had resigned before running for the Senate in 1926 and had never rejoined. Concluding his statement, he declared, "My discussion of this question is closed." Many Americans thought he should have stepped down from his position on the Supreme Court, but with the support of President Franklin D. Roosevelt, Black kept his seat and became a noted champion of equal rights and civil liberties.

During the 1920s, the Klan also achieved great political victories in the West and Midwest. Although it was crippled in California by outbreaks of violence, including a deadly shootout with police near Los Angeles, the order found a welcome reception in Colorado, as well as Oregon.

Like Oregon, Colorado was the home of a large number of white, native-born Protestants, who showed an extreme intolerance of other groups. In Denver, the Invisible Empire swelled its ranks by adopting the slogan, "Catholics, you are not Americans." One Klan leader built up his restaurant business by advertising, "We Serve Fish Every Day—Except Friday." Attracted primarily by the anti-Catholic propaganda, one out of every ten Denver residents joined the KKK. With this kind of power, Denver Klansmen soon served as mayor, city attorney, and police chief. In addition, many lesser offices were held by Klan members.

In 1924, the Invisible Empire captured control of Colorado's Republican party and put up an all-Klan ticket for the state's highest offices. The Grand Dragon of Colorado, Dr. John Galen Locke, declared that "the Klan will support no man in the coming election unless he signs his name on the dotted line to all the pledges and promises the Klan demands." Many politicians eagerly sided with the Invisible Empire in an election campaign dominated by the issue of the Klan. Although working through the Republican party, the Grand Dragon reminded the faithful, "We are not Republicans or Democrats but Klansmen."

The Klan swept the 1924 election in Colorado. A Klansman, Clarence Morley, was elected governor. Klan-supported candidates became U.S. senator, lieutenant governor, attorney general, state auditor, secretary of state, and state supreme court justice. Moreover, the Klan won control of one house of the state legislature. As governor, Morley made no effort to hide his ties to the Klan. He met regularly with Grand Dragon Locke, appointed Klansmen to office, and even led a parade of Klansmen through Denver, the state capital.

A Denver newspaper concluded that Grand Dragon Locke had in effect become the dictator of Colorado. "He may at his pleasure remove any officer in the state," the paper charged. "He may also suspend any man from the order without a hearing. . . . They either obey or are kicked out of the organization."

Although the Klan spread to every part of the United States in the early and mid 1920s, it was strongest in the Midwest. The states of Ohio, Indiana, Illinois, Michigan, and Wisconsin accounted for one third of the Klan's total membership. The two largest Realms in the country were Indiana and Ohio, each with a membership of over 250,000 Knights.

Kleagles found many native-born white Protestants in the Midwest who were worried about recent changes in the area. With the rise of industry and the growth of the cities came blacks from the South and immigrants from Europe in search of economic opportunity. Rapid social changes aroused racial and religious hatreds that were exploited by Klan recruiters who flooded the Midwest.

In Ohio, the Klan signed up between 200,000 and 400,000 Knights. Headquartered in Columbus, it won a number of local political victories and elected the mayors of Akron, Youngstown, Canton, and Warren. Yet the Ohio Klan failed in its attempts to capture statewide offices because of weak and divided leadership.

Across the border in Indiana, the Invisible Empire ran the state for several years. The man responsible for the most powerful Realm in Klandom was David C. Stephenson, Indiana's Grand Dragon. A born salesman, Steve—as he liked to be called—knew a sure thing when he saw it. He also showed he could bend with the wind—if power and money were at stake. Shortly after arriving in Evansville, Indiana, Stephenson ran for Congress in 1920 as a Democrat and a "wet" in favor of the sale of alcoholic beverages. Defeated by the opposition of the local Anti-Saloon League, he quickly became a "dry" Republican. He also joined the Ku Klux Klan and rose rapidly as a result of his abilities as an orator and organizer. By 1922, the thirty-one-year-old Stephenson was King Kleagle for Indiana, and his sales force had brought over 250,000 Hoosiers into the Klan. In return for helping Hiram Wesley Evans depose Imperial Wizard Simmons in 1922, Stephenson was put in charge of recruiting for twenty states from Maine to Nebraska.

Typically, the Indiana Klan appealed to deep-seated prejudices against Catholics, Jews, and blacks. However, Roman Catholics were the most numerous and most hated enemy of native-born Protestant Hoosiers, and Stephenson's Kleagles flooded the state with outrageous propaganda against Catholics. This included photographs of a church in Washington, D.C., that was alleged to be a new Vatican under construction for the pope's future home. The structure, actually a Protestant church, was supposedly placed on the heights above Washington so that the pope could fire artillery shells at the White House and the Capitol.

One Klansman, who got carried away by his own anti-Catholic rhetoric, told a crowd in North Manchester, Indiana, that the pope might arrive in town any day. "He may even be on the north-bound train tomorrow. He may! He may! Be warned! Prepare! America for Americans! Search everywhere for hidden enemies, vipers at the heart's blood of our sacred Republic! Watch the trains!" A mob of 1,500 people met the train the following day, and they held the only arriving passenger—a ladies' underwear salesman—until they were assured that he was not the pope in disguise.

Kluxing made Stephenson a millionaire. He owned a luxurious home, a ninety-eight-foot yacht, a fleet of automobiles, an airplane, and a private railroad car. He also had an office in Indianapolis that featured a bank of telephones, including a fake one supposedly linked directly to the White House.

"Stephenson took in enough within less than two years to enable him to live like a king," former Imperial Wizard Simmons once remarked. "His dream was to be the Mussolini of America."

Stephenson preferred to think of himself as Napoleon, but in any case he planned to become president of the United States. The most colorful Klansman in the nation always thought big, and he knew how to capture the public's attention.

On July 4, 1923, Stephenson was sworn in as Indiana's Grand Dragon at a Konklave in Kokomo that drew over 100,000 Klansmen. He made a spectacular entrance by arriving in an airplane that landed next to the rally. Armed bodyguards cleared a path through the crowd for the purple-robed Grand Dragon. Mounting the speakers' platform, Stephenson told the hushed multitude: "My worthy subjects, citizens of the Invisible Empire, Klansmen all, greetings. It grieves me to be late. The President of the United States kept me unduly long counselling upon vital matters of state. Only my plea that this is the time and place of my coronation obtained for me a surcease from his prayers for guidance." Stephenson then delivered an address on the need for "100 per cent Americanism." As he finished speaking, a coin was thrown toward him from the crowd. A wave of rings, watch chains, coins, and other valuables followed. The Grand Dragon's retainers gathered up the tribute and Stephenson departed, knowing he was the most powerful man in Indiana.

Stephenson's dreams of glory inevitably took the Klan into Indiana politics. Since Republicans already dominated the state, Stephenson set out to capture control of the Republican party in 1924. His well-oiled machine made the Republican state convention look like a Kloncilium. Klan-supported candidates for major offices won both the Republican primary and the general election in November. Stephenson himself did not run for office, preferring to remain the power behind the throne. But the Grand Dragon exercised tremendous influence over the governor, Edward Jackson, and the majority of the state legislature, which identified with the Invisible Empire. For good measure Stephenson's Klan also dominated the city of Indianapolis, including the mayor's office.

Stephenson's sense of power led to his famous declaration, "I am the law!" And he was—at least for a short time.

The Invisible Empire reached the peak of its political power in 1924. Nationwide, the success of the Ku Klux Klan appeared awesome, with notable victories not only in Indiana and Colorado, but also in Oklahoma, Kentucky, and Kansas. Perhaps the greatest proof of the Klan's drawing power came in the country's northernmost state, where the group helped elect Ralph Owen Brewster governor of Maine. Brewster, a Harvard-educated Yankee who never joined the Invisible Empire, won the Klan's endorsement by opposing public aid for parochial schools. The estimated 15,000 Klansmen in Maine undoubtedly made the crucial difference in putting Brewster in the governor's chair.

Although the Klan scored numerous local and state victories, it failed in its grasp for the White House. Nevertheless, it had considerable impact on the 1924 presidential campaign.

The setting for one of the great political battles of all time was the 1924 Democratic national convention, held in New York's Madison Square Garden. As Democrats gathered to nominate a presidential candidate, they divided on a number of issues, but the Klan aroused the most turmoil. Strong support for the Klan came from many southern and western states, such as Georgia, Florida, Mississippi, Texas, Oklahoma, and Kansas. The few known Klansmen at the convention included the chairman of the Georgia delegation, a national committeeman from Arkansas, and Senator Earle Mayfield of the Texas delegation. Outside the convention, Imperial Wizard Evans and assorted Grand Dragons set up headquarters in a nearby hotel to keep tabs on the Democrats' activities.

The two leading contenders for the presidential nomination symbolized the growing split in the Democratic party. Williams Gibbs McAdoo, the son-in-law of former President Woodrow Wilson, came to the convention as the favorite of the Klan and Prohibition forces because he was a "dry" who refused to attack the powerful Klan even though he himself was not a member. McAdoo's studied silence on the issue of the Klan won him the endorsement of such leading Knights as Senator Mayfield and Imperial Wizard Evans. The Klan's sworn enemy was New York's Governor Al Smith, a Roman Catholic and a "wet" opposed to Prohibition.

Another presidential hopeful, Alabama's Senator Oscar Underwood, carried the burden of the fight against the Invisible Empire. Although considered "the first statesman of the South," Underwood openly attacked the Klan as an antidemocratic force responsible for many of the South's problems. As a result, the Klan helped deny Underwood support in every southern state except his home state of Alabama. Senator Underwood arrived at the Democratic convention declaring he would make the Klan the number one issue.

Asked if he would introduce a plank in the Democratic platform condemning the secret order by name, Underwood responded: "The party is either for or against the Klan. Of course, we should name the Klan. Why not?"

The anti-Klan forces quickly got an opportunity to strike the first blow in the fight shaping up at Madison Square Garden. When the nominating process began with the alphabetical roll call of the states, an Alabama delegate nominated Senator Underwood and added that the party platform should condemn the "Ku Klux Klan." Upon hearing those three words, delegates went wild. The Alabama delegation, followed by New York and other northeastern states, poured into the aisles for an impromtu anti-Klan demonstration. Spurred on by spectators who cheered and the band, which played "America," delegates from a number of midwestern states joined the demonstration. Most southern and western delegates sat quietly fuming. In several divided delegations there was pushing and shoving when some members fought to take to the floor. Order was finally restored after twenty-five minutes, but the issue of the Klan did not disappear.

The showdown between the Klan and anti-Klan forces came in the debate over the party platform. The dispute began in the platform committee when Edmond Moore of Ohio proposed a plank pledging the Democratic party "to oppose any effort on the part of the Ku Klux Klan, or any organization, to interfere with the religious liberty or political freedom of any citizen." Defending the anti-Klan declaration, Moore argued, "If we do not destroy the Klan, it will destroy the Democratic party." While supporters of Underwood and Smith backed Moore's proposal, McAdoo's forces opposed citing the Klan by name in the platform. The policy of silence won approval from a majority in the platform committee, but anti-Klan delegates took the issue to the full convention.

The resulting debate ripped the Democratic party apart. Anti-Klan speakers brought the gallery of spectators to a fever pitch. The unexpected support of a young Georgia newspaper editor, Andrew D. Erwin of the Athens *Banner-Herald*, triggered the second anti-Klan demonstration by delegates who marched around Madison Square Garden with Erwin on their shoulders.

The old Democratic warhorse, William Jennings Bryan, then addressed the convention. Long recognized as a spokesman for rural America, the three-time nominee for president called for omitting the three words "Ku Klux Klan" from the platform. This suggestion brought forth a barrage of hisses and boos from New Yorkers who packed the galleries.

During the voting on the anti-Klan plank, some delegates came to blows. As fistfights broke out around the convention floor, only the presence of 1,000 New York City policemen prevented a full-scale riot among the delegates. Amid the confusion, the convention decided by a razor-thin margin of one vote not to mention the Ku Klux Klan by name in the party platform. Over half the votes in support of the Klan's position came from outside the South.

The Invisible Empire won the battle over the platform but lost the war to nominate McAdoo. The fight over the Klan made the split in the Democratic party so great that McAdoo and Smith were deadlocked, with neither able to get the necessary two-thirds majority needed for the party's nomination. After a record 103 ballots over a nine-day period, the weary delegates finally selected John W. Davis, a compromise candidate who had taken no position on the Klan.

As the longest party convention in American history finally came to an end, a boxing promoter remarked, "Of all the fights I ever pulled off in the old Garden, that was the best draw I ever saw."

The Democratic nominee went on to denounce the Invisible Empire in his presidential campaign. John W. Davis declared: "If any organization, no matter what it chooses to be called, whether Ku Klux Klan or by any other name, raises the standard of racial and religious prejudice or attempts to make racial origins or religious beliefs the test of fitness for public office, it does violence to the spirit of American institutions and must be condemned." Davis called on the Republican candidate, President Calvin Coolidge, to condemn the Klan also, but "Silent Cal" chose to live up to his nickname and avoid the issue.

Although the question of the KKK did arise during the campaign, the Klan had no visible impact on the final outcome. The majority of Americans were Republicans, and Coolidge easily won the election. The White House had proved beyond the reach of the Ku Klux Klan.

(above) Imperial Wizard Robert Shelton standing before a burning cross at a KKK rally in 1965. Shelton has headed the largest faction of Klansmen, the United Klans of America, since 1961.

(opposite, top) In August, 1925, some 40,000 Klansmen and Klanswomen marched through Washington, D.C., in one of the largest parades in the history of the nation's capital. (National Archives)

(opposite, bottom) Dr. Hiram Wesley Evans (left), a Dallas dentist, shown with J. M. Frazer (right) of the Sam Houston Klan No. 1. After deposing William Joseph Simmons, Dr. Evans served as Imperial Wizard of the Knights of the Ku Klux Klan, Inc., from 1923 until 1939. (National Archives)

As the civil rights movement grew, so too did violence against blacks. Shown here is Felton Turner, who in 1960 was abducted in Houston, Texas, by four men who beat him and carved the letters "KKK" across his stomach. (UPI)

(above) Michael Schwerner, Andrew Goodman and James Chaney were young civil rights workers killed near Philadelphia, Mississippi, in the summer of 1964. The murders were committed by members of the Original Knights of the Ku Klux Klan of Mississippi. (UPI)

(right) In 1964, Atlanta Klansmen protest the recent integration of a hotel, while a few blocks away, blacks picketed a segregated restaurant which refused to integrate. (UPI)

(above, left) Viola Liuzzo, a Detroit housewife and mother of five children, was killed by Klansmen after she took part in the 1965 civil rights march from Selma to Montgomery, Alabama. (UPI)

(above, right) Gary Thomas Rowe, Jr., was an FBI informant in the Ku Klux Klan, who helped convict three Klansmen of participating in the 1965 shooting death of Viola Liuzzo. Rowe himself was indicted in 1978 for allegedly taking part in the murder. (Wide World Photos)

(opposite, top) The burning of a giant cross, encircled by robed and hooded Klansmen, traditionally takes place at the end of outdoor Klan rallies. Shown here is the cross burning at a 1978 rally held by the United Klans of America in a cow pasture near Plant City, Florida. (Mary Duvendack)

(opposite, bottom) Civil rights leader Martin Luther King, Jr., pulling up a cross that was burned in front of his Atlanta home in 1960. The burning cross, symbol of the Ku Klux Klan, was used to threaten civil rights workers in the South. (UPI)

The Rev. James L. Betts, leader of a splinter Klan in Missouri, displays 1975 propaganda against busing to integrate schools. (UPI)

"Colonel" William Joseph Simmons, Imperial Wizard of the Knights of the Ku Klux Klan, Inc., which he founded in 1915 and which became the largest Klan in history during the 1920s. (UPI)

6 / The Klan Kollapses

THE LAST GREAT SHOW OF KLAN STRENGTH CAME IN AUGUST, 1925, when members of the Invisible Empire descended on Washington, D.C. Arriving from all directions, Klansmen and Klanswomen poured into the nation's capital to stage a well-publicized parade down Pennsylvania Avenue. Delegations, primarily from northern states like Pennsylvania, Ohio, and New Jersey, came in chartered trains and in private cars that carried flags with the coded Klan greeting "KIGY." ("Klansmen, I greet you"). Many of the Knights pitched tents on a thirteen-acre site that was billed as the "100 Per Cent American Camp." Although Catholic, Jewish, and black groups demanded that Washington ban the Klan march, the city refused as long as members of the Invisible Empire abided by a local law that prohibited the wearing of masks in public.

At the appointed hour on Saturday, August 8, 1925, the mammoth parade began. At the head of the long column was Imperial Wizard Hiram Wesley Evans, decked out in his purple satin robe with gold trimmings. Following him came some 40,000 Klansmen and Klanswomen in their white robes and hoods, but with their faces unmasked. Together they formed one of the largest parades in the history of the nation's capital. Marching twenty to twenty-five abreast, they passed in review for almost four hours. A friendly crowd, estimated at 200,000, lined the parade route and applauded as the Knights made their way to a rally at the Washington Monument.

The impressive demonstration was intended to show that the Invisible Empire had lost none of its strength. It appeared to achieve that end, since most observers were surprised by the large turnout. "The parade was grander and gaudier than anything the wizards had prophesied," one Klan opponent remarked. Yet even the spectacular parade could not conceal the fact that the power of the Ku Klux Klan was rapidly diminishing around the country—the empire was collapsing.

Klan membership had peaked by 1924. After that, Americans deserted the order as quickly as they had joined. A survey of the Klan by the *New York Times* concluded in 1926, "Everywhere it shows signs of dissolution; nowhere are there indications of gain." Congressional and state elections that year were a setback for the Klan, particularly in Colorado, Indiana, and Oregon, where it lost most of its political power. In Georgia, every candidate supported by the Klan was defeated. Texas membership fell from 100,000 in 1924 to 18,000 two years later, and the governor of Texas proclaimed the Klan "as dead as the proverbial doornail."

Even the Klan was forced to admit its growing weakness. In an attempt to rally the faithful in 1925, it observed: "The early church was bitterly persecuted, but it prospered. The Masons were bitterly persecuted, but they weathered the storm. The Klan is having its testing period. Will it survive? Let God and time answer."

Time answered quickly. By 1930, the Invisible Empire was truly almost invisible, counting less than 40,000 members nationally. Imperial Wizard Evans, in a gross understatement, declared, "There is some truth in reports of our weakness; we lost strength at certain points."

The story of the Klan's collapse is as complicated as that of its rise. Just as Americans joined it for many different reasons, so too they packed away their sheets for a wide variety of motives. The fact that they left the Klan so quickly and in such great numbers suggests a powerful combination of forces at work.

In part, a feeling of success undermined the Klan's appeal. By the mid-1920s, defenders of traditional America could take comfort in several victories over "alien threats." In 1924, Congress responded to the growing hatred of foreigners by severely restricting immigration into the United States. The National Origins Act limited the number of immigrants permitted into the country and effectively stopped the flood tide of Europeans, who had poured into the United States at the rate of over 1 million a year before World War I. Southern and Eastern Europeans were discriminated against through a quota system designed to keep down the flow that had previously brought great numbers of Catholics and Jews into the United States, and Asians were barred altogether.

At home, Protestants committed to the old-time religion defeated the forces of change in the famous Scopes trial. The 1925 court battle pitted William Jennings Bryan, spokesman for rural America, against Clarence Darrow, the toughest defense lawyer of his day. The two clashed in Dayton, Tennessee, where a local biology teacher, John T. Scopes, was tried for teaching Darwin's view of evolution. Scopes was specifically charged with violating a state law that prohibited the teaching of anything that conflicted with the literal view of creation as presented in the Bible. Darrow, acting as defense attorney for Scopes, scored a number of points against Bryan, who appeared for the prosecution, but traditionalists won the battle. Scopes was found guilty, and anti-evolution laws remained on the books of many states, especially in the South.

Prohibition, another defense of "100 per cent Americanism," also remained the law of the land throughout the 1920s, despite widespread violations. Furthermore, "dry" forces could point to a sharp reduction in the consumption of alcohol as evidence of their victory over "demon rum."

Indeed, developments of the 1920s increasingly soothed the fears of people who had briefly seen the Ku Klux Klan as the last defense of nineteenth-century America. Prosperity helped ease the anxieties that gripped America after World War I. Model T Fords and electric appliances made twentieth century life more acceptable. The new symbol of America was President Calvin Coolidge (1923–1929), a decidedly nineteenth-century man born in Plymouth Notch, Vermont. A product of strict New England Puritanism, Coolidge neither smoke nor drank. He made a point of napping every afternoon and getting to bed by ten every evening. With prosperity and Coolidge, what did Americans have to worry about?

Since the Klan appealed to people's fears, it undoubtedly suffered from the changed climate of the period. However, Klan leaders made things worse by engaging in corrupt and criminal conduct.

Almost from the beginning, the Klan had been weakened by evidence of immoral and illegal activities committed by its officials. Klansmen also fought among themselves.

In 1927, Imperial Wizard Evans resorted to a law suit to quell open rebellion in the Realm of Pennsylvania. That state had the largest Klan membership in the Northeast— with some 150,000 Knights. However, the group was deeply divided, preventing it from winning political power. Internal dissension finally resulted in the Grand Dragon's banishment of several Klaverns. When the outlawed Klansmen continued to operate, Imperial Wizard Evans requested a federal court order barring the rebels from using the Klan name. Evans also filed a $100,000 damage suit designed to scare his Pennsylvania opponents into submission.

The rebel Klansmen fought back with a countersuit. They charged state and national leaders with engaging in such illegal practices as misusing funds, intimidating voters, interrupting religious services, and causing "menacing riots of murder, lynching and bloodshed." In support of these accusations, Pennsylvania Klansmen testified to having participated in kidnappings and beatings "under the direct authorization of the principal officers of the state."

A former Kleagle and Kligrapp of the Pennsylvania Klan summed up his experiences in the Invisible Empire by telling the court, "The provision of the national charter calling for a benevolent, religious and charitable institution is a joke; it is run entirely for profit."

Although top Klan leaders denied these accusations, the federal judge hearing the case threw out their suit. After hearing all the evidence of lawlessness, the judge ruled that the KKK, "stigmatized as it is by its unlawful acts and conduct, could hardly hope for judicial assistance in a court of the United States." The Klan, once billed as a defender of law and order, stood publicly condemned as unlawful.

Evans' plan had clearly backfired. Instead of bringing order to the Pennsylvania Realm, his lawsuit had revealed the dismal inner operations of the Klan. Newspapers had a field day exposing the charges and countercharges thrown by Klansmen. Such publicity further damaged the hooded order's tarnished image. Within a year, Pennsylvania's Invisible Empire declined to only 10,000 members.

Indiana provided the worst example of Klan criminality. Shortly after Grand Dragon

David C. Stephenson reached the peak of his power in 1923, his empire began to crumble. First, he was banished from the Klan for conduct "unbecoming a Klansman" as a result of his questionable relations with women. Denying the charges, he fought back. He called Hoosier Klansmen to headquarters in Indianapolis and got himself elected Grand Dragon in defiance of Imperial Wizard Evans. With Stephenson still in control, Imperial leaders apparently attempted to frame him for a crime. Early in 1925, a woman claiming to be his long-lost wife showed up in Indianapolis and filed a suit charging that Stephenson had deserted her and failed to support her child.

Meanwhile, Stephenson himself had committed a much greater outrage. When a young state employee, Madge Oberholtzer, refused to accompany him on a trip to Chicago, Stephenson had three men force her into a private room on a Chicago-bound train. Steve then assaulted her, and in despair she swallowed poison, resulting in her death several weeks later. Before she died, Oberholtzer dictated a statement naming Stephenson as her assailant.

Stephenson claimed it was a frame-up by his enemies in the Klan, but an Indiana jury disagreed. After a month-long trial, he was found guilty of second-degree murder for having driven Madge Oberholtzer to commit suicide. The judge sentenced him to life imprisonment in 1925.

Stephenson remained confident. He boasted that he would get a pardon from Governor Ed Jackson, the man put in office by his Klan. When the pardon was not forthcoming, Stephenson turned on his former associates. He disclosed the location of two "little black boxes" that contained his private papers. The contents provided enough evidence of corrupt practices to send the mayor of Indianapolis and several other officials to jail. Governor Jackson was indicted for bribery, but he was saved from conviction because the statute of limitations had run out.

From his jail cell, Stephenson declared: "I should have been put in jail for my political activities, but I am not guilty of murder." Perhaps not, but his violation of legal and moral standards doomed the Indiana Klan. Indeed, the entire Invisible Empire was discredited by his sensational downfall. In the light of such activities, the Klan could hardly claim to be a defender of morality or Americanism.

In addition to internal decay, a variety of outside forces brought the Ku Klux Klan to its

66

knees in the 1920s. Newspaper attacks, especially those from New York papers like the *World*, initially had little impact on the Klan, but local newspapers gradually helped turn the tide of public opinion against the organization. In several communities where it was strong, courageous newspaper editors were the first to speak out against the Klan.

The leading opponent of the Georgia Klan was Julian Harris, editor of the Columbus *Enquirer-Sun* and son of Joel Chandler Harris, famed author of the Uncle Remus stories. While other Georgia newspapers, especially in Atlanta, remained silent, Julian Harris singlehandedly chipped away at the order. The *Enquirer-Sun* was the only Georgia newspaper to reprint the New York *World*'s exposé of the Klan. Harris also taunted his readers with editorials based on the popular slogan, "It's great to be a Georgian."

"Is it great to be a citizen of a state which is the proud parent of a cowardly hooded order founded and fostered by men who have been proved liars, drunkards, blackmailers, and murderers?" asked Harris editorially. "Is it great to be a citizen of a state whose governor is a member of and subservient to that vicious masked gang, and whose officials are either members or in sympathy with it? Is it great to be a citizen of such a state? Is it great to be a Georgian?"

When an Atlanta minister and chaplain of the Klan was arrested for driving while under the influence of alcohol, Harris featured the story in an editorial entitled, "The Drunken Kludd."

He persisted in attacking the Klan despite a decline in circulation and threats from the Invisible Empire. Soon other Georgia newspapers joined his crusade, and in 1925 Julian Harris won a Pulitzer prize for public service—the highest tribute that can be paid to a newspaperman. By then, the Klan's influence was declining in Georgia, and Harris could take some credit for exposing the hooded order.

In neighboring Alabama, Grover Cleveland Hall, editor of the Montgomery *Advertiser*, led the anti-Klan campaign. Hall publicized the violence that plagued the Alabama Klan. According to Hall, "the chivalrous South" had a new means of dealing with a "loose" woman: "We bend her over a barrel, or a log, or tie her to a tree and beat the hell out of her—we Southern gents." Like Julian Harris, Hall helped reveal the truth about the Invisible Empire, and he too won a Pulitzer prize for his strong stand.

In Memphis, Tennessee, the largest newspaper in the region, the *Commercial-Appeal*, consistently attacked the Klan. Slashing editorials and scathing cartoons ridiculed the society. "Law and order have not yet gotten to the point where they must hide behind closed doors and mask their faces," observed one editorial. A Klan newspaper complained that the *Commercial-Appeal* was one of "the three most vicious anti-Klan newspapers in the country." That explains in part why the Invisible Empire failed in its attempt to capture political control of Memphis. A Pulitzer prize was awarded to the *Commercial-Appeal* for "its courageous attitude in the publication of cartoons and the handling of news in reference to the operation of the Ku Klux Klan."

Although most newspapers remained silent or even supported the Klan, anti-Klan editors won national attention and helped undermine the order in their areas. Once it began its decline, the press sealed its fate by showing wavering Knights what the group was really like.

During the 1920s, the Klan was subjected not only to verbal abuse but also to physical assault in some areas. Bootleggers, for example, did not take kindly to the Klan's attempts to enforce Prohibition. When New Jersey's Invisible Empire declared war on local bootleggers, the rumrunners formed a defense council and publicly threatened to "shoot to kill" anyone other than a policeman who interfered with their illegal traffic in liquor.

Roman Catholics also did not take lightly the Klan's vicious attacks on their religion. In major cities like New York, Boston, and Pittsburgh that had heavily Catholic populations, Klansmen risked life and limb if they dared show their masked faces in public. The Invisible Empire could not even count on police protection in large eastern cities, since many of the policemen were anti-Klan Catholics. When Kleagles first arrived in New York City, Mayor John F. Hylan issued the following order to his police commissioner: "I desire you to treat this group of racial and religious haters as you would the Reds and bomb throwers. Drive them out of the city." Several years later, 1,000 Klansmen broke into a Memorial Day parade held in New York's borough of Queens. The white-robed and hooded Knights succeeded in covering the parade route, but they had to run a gauntlet of police and spectators who tried to stop them. A riot nearly resulted as Klansmen were attacked and five of their number were arrested.

In New Jersey, over 60,000 people joined the Klan, but they met stiff opposition in several cities. A minister was arrested in Paterson for passing out posters that declared, MEN AND WOMEN, KEEP THE ROMAN MENACE OUT. Newark's police chief threatened to shoot any Klansman who broke the law. Many towns denied parade permits to the secret order. When the mayor of Atlantic City called for an anti-Klan vigilance committee, 4,000 local residents turned out. Violence erupted in Perth Amboy, where thousands of people besieged a meeting of several hundred Klansmen. The anti-Klan rioters mauled the Knights as police tried to get them to safety. The badly beaten Klansmen barely escaped alive.

A mob screaming, "To hell with the Klan!" and "Hurrah for the Irish!" attacked Klansmen at a rally near New Castle, Delaware. Over fifty of the outnumbered Knights were injured escaping from a field where they had tried to burn a cross.

The worst anti-Klan violence occurred in Pennsylvania. In the summer of 1923, some 10,000 Klansmen gathered outside Carnegie, a steel town near Pittsburgh, to hear a speech by Imperial Wizard Evans. A march through the town was to follow, but the mayor refused to grant a permit on the grounds that violence would probably result, since Carnegie was equally divided between Protestants and Catholics. The assembled Klansmen decided to march anyway. As the hooded Knights entered the town, they were met by an anti-Klan mob throwing bricks and bottles. When the Klansmen pushed ahead, shots rang out and a Klansman fell dead. Retreating Knights were kept from returning to Carnegie by Imperial Wizard Evans.

Several months later, the Klan put on a show of strength at Lilly, a largely Catholic mining town near Altoona, Pennsylvania. Knights from the surrounding area poured into Lilly on a chartered train. After burning a cross, Klansmen exchanged shots with anti-Klan protestors and a Klansman lost his life.

Such violence, although often provoked by the Invisible Empire, led to complaints from the hooded order. A Klan newspaper protested against "the reign of terror, launched to intimidate Protestants." By 1924, the group charged that "the list of outrages against Klansmen is so long that it would take weeks to compile even an incomplete list."

Legal means were also used to curb the Klan during the 1920s. In Chicago, the city council appointed a committee made up of a Catholic, a Jew, and a black to recommend legislation on the Klan. The result was a law forbidding city employees from joining the organization. Illinois passed a state law forbidding the wearing of masks in public. New York State enacted even stiffer anti-Klan laws under the leadership of the country's major Catholic politician, Governor Al Smith. The state required the Invisible Empire to file membership lists, which were then made available to the public. Furthermore, New York barred the Klan from taking part in politics.

Despite the many external pressures, the Ku Klux Klan collapsed largely as a result of internal weaknesses. Corruption, division, and criminality soon disillusioned the millions of Knights who had joined in hopes of defending "Americanism." Once the Klan itself appeared "un-American," it could no longer hold most of its followers. By 1930, the Klan was barely visible. Never again would it regain the power it had temporarily achieved during the early 1920s. However, the Invisible Empire remained alive, as did the deep-rooted prejudices that had produced it.

7/The Depression Years

AFTER THE REVERSALS OF THE LATE 1920s, THE GREAT DEPRESSION was another blow to the fortunes of the Ku Klux Klan. With mounting unemployment and growing poverty after 1929, Klan membership fees became a luxury few Americans could afford. Yet 50,000 to 100,000 Knights kept the Invisible Empire alive during the 1930s. There hooded bigots proved that even a severely crippled Klan could still cause trouble and capture national attention.

Imperial Wizard Evans spent the decade trying to stir life into the Klan. Traveling across the country, he lectured widely, apparently searching for the issue that would revive his fallen empire. The Klan leadership tried in vain to blame the widespread unemployment on aliens, who supposedly took jobs from American citizens. But few people took seriously the Klan's proposal to cure the depression by deporting all aliens. The sagging spirit of Americans could hardly have been boosted by the Klan's New Year's greeting for 1931:

> And here's hoping
> That you keep
> Smiling Through
> 1931 with the Ku Klux Klan.

In the North, the Invisible Empire was primarily a fraternal order during the depression. Local Klaverns remained out of sight except when members donned their white robes for parades and cross burnings. Uniformed Klansmen regularly held outdoor ceremonies on New York's Long Island and in the Hudson River Valley town of Peekskill. Cities in New Jersey, Ohio, and Michigan also had occasional Klan rallies. These gatherings rarely attracted as many as 1,000 Knights—a far cry from the great rallies of the 1920s that drew 50,000.

Meanwhile, southern Klansmen continued to resort to violence. Hooded night riders still tried to enforce their version of morality with a whip. The worst mob violence occurred in Florida and Georgia, which had the strongest Realms in the country. In St. Petersburg, Florida, a Klan "wrecking crew" terribly mutilated a man who supposedly violated some Klan standard of conduct. In Miami, almost 200 white-robed Klansmen raided a night club, where they beat employees, smashed furniture, and ordered the place closed. Georgia Klansmen flogged the white owner of a movie theater that catered to blacks. An Atlanta barber was whipped to death by hooded men.

As usual, Imperial leaders denied that the Klan was involved in any of these illegal activities. They pointed to the lack of indictments as proof of the Klan's innocence. However, in some areas the lack was due to the fact that the Invisible Empire still dominated the law enforcement system. Nearly the entire police force in Greenville, South Carolina, was composed of Klansmen. Three deputy sheriffs in Fulton County, Georgia, admitted belonging to the secret order. In both Miami and Tampa, Florida, some city officials worked closely with the Klan.

To ensure white supremacy in the South, the Ku Klux Klan tried to keep blacks from voting. On the eve of a local election in Starke, Florida, white-robed and hooded Knights swept through the black area of town, where they burned crosses and left notes warning blacks "to stay out of Bradford County politics or take the consequences." In Miami, some fifty carloads of uniformed Klansmen invaded the city's black section and left cards signed "K.K.K." with the message, "Niggers stay away from the polls."

Nationally, the Invisible Empire fixed on anti-Communism as the way to attract new members in the 1930s. It continued to complain about Catholics, Jews, and blacks, but Communism became the root of all evil—opposed to God, the family, motherhood, white supremacy, and "Americanism." "The doctrines of Klankraft and of Communism are diametrically opposed," the secret order proclaimed, "and a battle to the finish must be fought." By 1935, the Invisible Empire found "strong evidence that Communism is making steady progress in undermining American civilization."

The Klan's chief evidence of alleged Communist infiltration was President Franklin Roosevelt's New Deal. Elected in 1932, the Democratic president supported a wide variety of popular reforms that extended federal aid to the unemployed, farmers, and laborers. In the midst of the worst economic crisis in their history, most Americans approved New Deal programs like Social Security, but the Klan attacked "the whole New Deal house of Socialist-Communist laws." Even worse in the eyes of Klansmen, Roosevelt's appointees included many Catholics and Jews and some blacks. These appointments seemed proof positive that the New Deal was inspired by Communists.

During the presidential election year of 1936, the Klan advocated the following six-point program:

1. Deport Undesirable Aliens
2. Drive Out Communism
3. Maintain Constitutional Government
4. Keep Church and State Separate
5. Buy American Made Products
6. Preserve White Supremacy

"Communism must be stamped out," one Kleagle told an audience of Klansmen. "The New Deal has become communistic and I feel certain that the American public will rise in protest and soundly defeat President Roosevelt at the next general election."

Never was the Klan more wrong. In 1936, Roosevelt was re-elected by a record margin in which he carried forty-six of the forty-eight states. Clearly, the overwhelming majority of Americans approved of FDR and his New Deal.

However, local Klaverns made the 1930s truly hard times for Communists or anyone considered a Communist. As usual, the South led the way in using terror to back up the Klan's program. In Dallas, armed Klansmen kidnapped and flogged two Communists for speaking out against the segregation and lynching of blacks. Knights in Birmingham, Alabama, flooded the city with a pamphlet that proclaimed: "Negroes of Birmingham, the Klan is watching you. Tell the Communists to get out of town. They mean only trouble for you, for Alabama is a good place for good Negroes and a bad place for Negroes who believe in racial equality. Report Communistic activities to the Ku Klux Klan, Box 661, Birmingham."

Even non-Communists fell victim to the Klan's anti-Communist crusade. In Tampa, Florida, police acting without a warrant raided a meeting of Modern Democrats, a small local group that had run candidates for office on a mildly socialist platform. The Modern Democrats "radical" ideas included free hospital care for the poor and public ownership of utilities like gas and electricity. After briefly questioning five Modern Democrats about alleged "Communist activities," Tampa police turned over three of them to a waiting gang of Klansmen. The three Modern Democrats were kidnapped, whipped, and tarred and feathered. The leader of the Modern Democrats, Joseph Shoemaker, was so badly beaten that he died a week later.

A national campaign for punishment of the floggers led to the indictment of eleven men for kidnapping and assault. All of the men arrested, including several Klansmen, had worked for Tampa's police department. The police chief himself was charged with trying to cover up for his men.

The Tampa Klan used the flogging as part of a recruiting effort. A leaflet issued right after the brutal attack asserted that "Communism Must Go" and proclaimed, THE KU KLUX KLAN RIDES AGAIN. The leaflet concluded with an appeal for help in the "last ditch" effort to stamp out Communism.

Much to the surprise of everyone, a jury found five of the policemen guilty of kidnapping. One juror commented, "Communism and all that stuff had nothing to do with the case." Another, a former deputy sheriff, told reporters: "What got us was the way those policemen, supposed to be the law enforcement officers, went right out and participated in an unlawful act." However, the policemen ultimately went free. The

Florida Supreme Court overturned the guilty verdict on a minor technicality, and later trials resulted in acquittals.

Unfortunately, the failure to punish criminals in the Klan encouraged other Knights to violence. In the late 1930s, the leading target of the Invisible Empire became union organizers. Stimulated by a rising economy and protective New Deal legislation, unions sought to sign up new members around the country. The campaign was led by the newly formed Committee of Industrial Organizations (CIO—later, the name was changed to Congress of Industrial Organizations). In the South, the CIO confronted opposition not only from businessmen but also from Klansmen, who were convinced that all labor organizers were Communists. After all, Imperial Wizard Evans had said that the CIO was "infested with Communists." That statement amounted to a declaration of war for Knights of the Invisible Empire. "The CIO is a subversive, radical, Red organization," a Florida Klansman asserted, "and we'll fight fire with fire." This attitude meant Klan threats, cross burnings, and ultimately attacks on union representatives. When the CIO's Textile Workers Organizing Committee arrived in Greenville, South Carolina, posters suddenly appeared around town declaring: "C.I.O. is Communism. Communism Will Not Be Tolerated. Ku Klux Klan Rides Again." In Atlanta, Klansmen who flogged a labor organizer bragged, "We're going to break up those damn unions."

The Klankraft practiced during the depression years failed to reverse the order's sagging fortunes. The shortage of money and the excess of violence combined to keep the Klan's membership well under 100,000 Knights.

By the end of the decade, Imperial Wizard Evans acted increasingly like a figure in a comic opera. Hard times forced Evans to sell the Klan's Imperial Palace in Atlanta. The former headquarters then wound up in the hands of the Catholic Diocese, which made it part of the new Cathedral of Christ the King. At the formal dedication in 1939, Bishop O'Hara of Atlanta invited the Imperial Wizard to attend the ceremonies. Evans accepted and was photographed standing with Bishop O'Hara and Cardinal Dougherty of Philadelphia. Two months later an Imperial Klonvokation of Klansmen removed Evans as Imperial Wizard. Evans claimed that he had wanted to step down, but whether or not he had, the state of the Klan and his appearance at a Catholic ceremony sealed his fate.

The new Imperial Wizard was James A. Colescott, a stocky, forty-two-year-old former veterinarian from Terre Haute, Indiana. Dr. Colescott had joined the Klan in 1923 and had served as an assistant to David C. Stephenson, the Grand Dragon of Indiana, who was later sentenced to life imprisonment. Colescott had moved up in Klandom, serving as Grand Dragon of Ohio and finally as chief assistant to Evans in Atlanta.

Imperial Wizard Colescott promised an "administration of action" to revive the Invisible Empire. He undertook speaking tours and sent out Kleagles with the traditional anti-Catholic, anti-Semitic, anti-black, and anti-foreign-born message of hate. A brief spurt in membership followed. In 1940, Colescott boasted a 50 percent jump in membership during his first year of leadership, but the actual figure was much less than the 500,000 claimed by the Imperial Wizard.

In any case, Klan activity virtually ceased in 1942 as a result of World War II. National unity temporarily overcame Klan bigotry as Colescott even asked to join Catholic and Jewish groups in patriotic programs. For the first time since the previous World War, the Invisible Empire disappeared from public view. Without disclosing the exact strength of the Klan, Colescott admitted that the group had "very few paid-up members."

Under pressure from the federal government, the Invisible Empire officially went out of business in 1944. That year the Bureau of Internal Revenue filed a suit against the Klan for back taxes of $685,000 on profits earned during the prosperous 1920s. To escape financial responsibility, a Klonvokation of Knights assembled in Atlanta, and in April, 1944, they "repealed all decrees, vacated all offices, voided all charters, and relieved every Klansman of any obligation whatever."

Explaining this turn of events, former Imperial Wizard Colescott later declared: "It was that nigger-lover Roosevelt and that Jew Morgenthau who was his Secretary of the Treasury who did it! I was sitting in my office in the Imperial Palace in Atlanta one day, just as pretty as you please, when the Revenuers knocked on my door and said they had come to collect three-quarters of a million dollars that the Government just figured out the Klan owed as taxes earned during the 1920s. . . . We had to sell our assets and hand over proceeds to the Government and go out of business. Maybe the Government can make something out of the Klan—I never could."

The Knights of the Ku-Klux Klan, Inc., the creation of Colonel William J. Simmons in

1915, had officially gone out of business. However, the religious and racial hatreds that had produced the Klan remained. So, too, did the white sheets, which could be brought out of the closets of former Klansmen whenever the situation demanded.

8 / Postwar Kluxers

IN THE SPRING OF 1946, LESS THAN A YEAR AFTER THE END OF WORLD War II, a call went out to Georgia Klansmen. "For five years you have asked for it—begged for it—here it is: A PUBLIC NATURALIZATION-IN-ROBES ON STONE MOUNTAIN, GEORGIA (the birthplace of the Klan). Get Your ROBES Laundered," the order read. "A CLASS OF 500 IS READY. America is calling every White Man, who has red blood, into the fight. WHITE SUPREMACY is threatened on every hand. YOU CANNOT FAIL." A postscript reminded Knights, "If you have not paid your 1946 dues get in touch with your Kligrapp [secretary] at once."

On the appointed night, a mob of Klansmen climbed to the top of Stone Mountain for the naturalization (initiation) ceremony. The way was lit by a fiery cross, measuring 200 by 300 feet, on the side of the mountain. A shortage of hoods forced hundreds of Knights to wear handkerchief masks. However, in all other respects the initiation followed the pattern set down by Colonel Simmons in 1915.

The new leader of the Ku Klux Klan was Dr. Samuel Green, an Atlanta obstetrician. A short, fifty-six-year-old man with glasses and a moustache, Dr. Green had joined the Invisible Empire in 1918. When the national Klan organization officially disbanded in 1944, Green had kept its spirit alive by creating an informal group called the Association of Georgia Klans. After the end of World War II, Green emerged as spokesman for the Klan, calling himself Grand Dragon of the Georgia Klan.

The time looked ripe for a revival of the Ku Klux Klan, especially in the South. First and foremost, World War II had sparked new interest in civil rights among American blacks. Aroused by wartime rhetoric emphasizing liberty and freedom for peoples around the world, blacks demanded a measure of equality at home, where they were segregated by law and denied the right to vote in the South. Even the federal government discriminated against blacks by segregating them in the Army and excluding them entirely from the Marine Corps. The Red Cross accepted an old racist myth in refusing so-called "black blood." Angered by such hypocrisy in the midst of a war for freedom, blacks launched a "Double V" campaign—victory for democracy at home and abroad. Black groups successfully pressured President Roosevelt into issuing an executive order banning discrimination in war-related industries. The president also created the Fair Employment Practices Committee (FEPC) to enforce the order. After Roosevelt's death, attempts were made to establish the FEPC as a permanent federal agency, but Southerners in Congress blocked the move.

Meanwhile, the U.S. Supreme Court struck a blow at restrictions that kept most blacks from voting in the South. In 1944, the Court ruled that political parties could not bar blacks from voting in primary elections. Until then, the so-called "white primary" had been used to keep blacks from participating in Democratic party primaries, where most election contests were decided in the solidly Democratic South. Although the removal of the white primary helped blacks, other barriers to voting remained. One was the poll tax—a fee required in order to cast a ballot. Under growing federal pressure, several southern states, including Georgia, repealed the poll tax by the end of World War II.

Peacetime also brought several other developments that troubled white Southerners. Some European refugees, especially Jews uprooted by the war, were permitted to emigrate to the United States. Peace also gave labor unions an opportunity to flex their muscles, and many looked at unorganized southern workers as labor's Achilles' heel. Unless the South was organized, northern companies would continue to flee southward in search of cheap labor. In 1946, both the American Federation of Labor (AFL) and the Congress of Industrial Organizations (CIO) created "Operation Dixie," a campaign that sent hundreds of labor organizers into the South.

Frightened by the impending upheaval, former Klansmen revived the ideas of the old Ku Klux Klan in hopes of stemming the new forces of change. Dr. Samuel Green, Georgia's Grand Dragon, sounded the alarm in an appeal directed at the rising fears of southern whites.

"The whole country has been flooded with Jewish refugees, and the Catholic church membership grows by leaps and bounds, even in the South where most fathers would rather see their daughters dead than married to a papist. And the uppity niggahs! Since the war they're even trying to abolish Jim Crow [segregation] laws, with their talk of equal rights. Already the poll tax has been abolished in Georgia, and in other Southern states Northern agitators are paying poll taxes for the blacks so they may vote alongside white folks. These same agitators are threatening Southern economic conditions. But I'll tell you this—no CIO or AFL carpetbagging organizers, or any other damned Yankees are going to come into the South and tell Southerners how to run either their businesses or their niggahs, nor shout that the niggah is equal to the white. The white man was born supreme. We won't tolerate any alliance between niggahs, Jews, Catholics and labor organizers either. We didn't want to be reconstructed, and we don't want to be organized! The Klan rides again!"

The times had changed since the 1920s, but not the Klan's message. The order was still anti-Catholic, anti-Semitic, antiblack, antiforeign and antiunion.

A sudden outburst of terrorism showed that Klan tactics also remained unchanged in the years after World War II. Burning crosses and verbal threats forced a Jewish storeowner out of business in a suburb of Chattanooga, Tennessee. A black union organizer was kidnapped and beaten by masked Klansmen in Georgia. A black war veteran was flogged in Mississippi for trying to register to vote.

Despite some signs of Klan activity in Ohio, Michigan, and California, most of the postwar surge was centered in the South. Asked why the Invisible Empire was largely inactive in northern states, Grand Dragon Green replied: "There's such an enormous foreign population there, Klansmen have to stay under cover."

Even in the South, the Klan made little headway in its recruiting campaign. A number of obstacles handicapped the attempt to revive the order. For one thing, the federal government still claimed that the old Knights of the Ku-Klux Klan, Inc., owed over $685,000 in back taxes. That meant Dr. Green could not renew the old charter of the Klan without facing a federal tax collector. When Dr. Green tried to evade the federal government by taking out a Georgia charter for his Association of Georgia Klans in 1946, the state immediately moved to revoke the charter, thereby preventing the Klan from conducting business as a legal fraternal organization. Georgia's attorney general charged that the Klan tried "to enforce its doctrines upon the State by violence, terrorism and hate." After a year of legal maneuvering, the Georgia Klan lost its state charter. Similar action was taken against the Klan in New York, New Jersey, and California.

Dismissing the importance of the Klan's legal problems, Grand Dragon Green declared that "the Klan was here yesterday, is here today and will be here forever."

Although Green's group could continue as an informal organization, it had a real problem. Without a corporate charter, the Georgia Klan no longer had an exclusive right to use the Klan's name or the practices of Klankraft. This meant anyone could organize a group called the Ku Klux Klan and charge initiation fees for membership.

Free enterprise and the profit motive splintered Klandom. A month after Green lost his charter, a Birmingham roofing contractor, William H. Morris, got an Alabama charter for the "Federated Ku Klux Klans of Alabama, Inc." The new self-styled Imperial Wizard was careful to say that his group had no legal tie with the old Klan, which had the enormous tax bill. "We have no connection with the old Klan, which has been defunct for some years," Morris stated, "but our basic principles are the same—the protection of the chastity of white womanhood and white supremacy."

Dr. Green had nothing but contempt for competing Klan groups, or "bolshevik Klans" as he referred to them. However, he could do nothing to prevent their spread across the South.

Weakened by legal problems, the postwar Klan confronted disinterest or intense dislike among most Southerners. The resistance to a revival of the Invisible Empire was led by courageous newspaper editors like Ralph McGill of the Atlanta *Constitution*. McGill wrote that Klan organizers "live a soft life. All they do is keep the suckers aroused about 'Niggers, Catholics, Jews, Communists' and so on." McGill thought even less of the "sheeted jerks" who joined the Klan. "The order attracts hoodlums. At least seventy percent of the Atlanta membership have police records ranging all the way from public drunkenness and disorderly conduct and robbery, to assault with intent to murder."

Southern clergymen also spoke out against the group. The Baptist church, which had supplied many members for the old Klan, openly attacked attempts to revive it. Condemning the Klan's misuse of religious symbols, one Baptist minister declared: "The Cross is to be borne, not burned." An association of Methodist ministers in Atlanta branded the Klan a "cowardly anti-Christian mob."

The federal government joined the campaign against the Klan. As soon as it reappeared in 1946, the FBI began investigating charges that Klansmen had violated federal civil rights laws. No indictments resulted, but Klansmen undoubtedly were more cautious knowing that the FBI was on their trail.

The Klan's image was further tarnished in 1947 when the Attorney General of the United States included it in a list of groups designated as "totalitarian, fascist, communist or subversive." After years of claiming to defend "100 per cent Americanism," the Klan was thus grouped with the Communist party and branded "un-American."

To make matters worse, the Klan's innermost secrets were exposed by spies who infiltrated the organization. The most troublesome spy was Stetson Kennedy, a southern writer who joined the postwar Klan in Georgia and lived to tell the story in a book entitled *I Rode with the Ku Klux Klan*. Kennedy also supplied the Georgia Bureau of Investigation with information used in the lawsuit that lifted the Klan's charter.

Kennedy was so trusted by the Atlanta Klavern that he was invited to join its elite flogging squad, the Klavalier Klub. During his initiation into the Klavalier Klub, he was told by the Klavern Night Hawk that "we Klavaliers serve as the secret police of the KKK and are entrusted with carrying out all 'direct-line' activity." In case there was any doubt what that meant, Kennedy had to "swear to provide [himself] with a good gun and plenty of ammunition, so as to be ready when the nigger starts trouble." He was also warned of the penalty for betraying secrets of the Klan—"Death at the hands of a Brother." To ensure that no one in the flogging squad would inform on the others, every Klavalier had to take a turn with the whip.

"In the Klavalier Klub," the Night Hawk said pointedly, "every man takes his turn with the whip on every job. That way, there's less chance of anybody ever doing any talking."

"There's a certain knack to using that bullwhip," the Night Hawk told Kennedy. "A time or two we have killed men with it when we wasn't aimin' to. You'll catch on to it soon enough!"

In order to protect his cover, Stetson Kennedy participated in several flogging sessions, but he later testified in court against Klansmen. He also helped prevent some beatings by warning the authorities in advance. Perhaps most important, Kennedy exposed the violent nature of the Klan.

Even Superman joined the crusade against the Klan. On the basis of information privately supplied by Stetson Kennedy, the popular radio hero devoted a month to pursuing Kluxers. Atlanta Klansmen were almost driven crazy by hearing their own children repeat the secret Klan password, which they heard from Superman. As quickly as Klansmen changed the password, Stetson Kennedy relayed the new one to writers of *Superman*.

Despite many obstacles, the Invisible Empire appeared to make some headway in 1948. That year President Harry S Truman provided it with an explosive issue when he came out in favor of expanded civil rights for blacks during his election campaign. Angry southern Democrats deserted their party in droves, and the Klan tried to exploit the race issue in its usual fashion.

"If anyone wants to sit and eat with niggers that's their business," Grand Dragon Green declared in Georgia. But he added, "God Himself segregated the races." Denouncing President Truman's civil rights program and reviving images of Reconstruction, Green warned Southerners: "Again you will see Yankee bayonets trying to force social and racial equality between the black and white races. If that happens there are those among you who will see blood flow in these streets."

Taking their cue from the Grand Dragon, Klansmen tried to intimidate black voters in the South. On the eve of state elections in Georgia, masked Knights paraded through small towns and burned crosses. In Wrightsville, Klan threats kept all 400 registered black voters from appearing at the polls.

"We reaffirm our loyalty to the Constitution, and vow to uphold the laws, but there are some things beyond the law," Dr. Green told 300 robed and hooded followers at Wrightsville. "No matter what the law says in this country, it's still wrong to allow a Negro to vote in a white man's primary."

This appeal to lawlessness brought new recruits to Klandom. At one ceremony during the summer of 1948, Green's Klan inducted about 700 men and 12 women into the Invisible Empire. The initiation, probably the largest since the 1920s, attracted Klansmen to Georgia's Stone Mountain from the neighboring states of Florida, Alabama, and Tennessee.

The Klan helped elect Herman Talmadge governor of Georgia in 1948. The following year, Grand Dragon Green claimed to be a lieutenant colonel and aide-de-camp on Governor Talmadge's personal staff. Asked if that was true, Talmadge responded evasively, "I don't know."

The Invisible Empire was slowly gaining momentum during the late 1940s. Grand Dragon Green claimed in 1949 that his Association of Georgia Klans had about 20,000 members in 140 Klaverns in Georgia, South Carolina, Florida, Alabama, and Tennessee. The figure of 20,000 may have been inflated, since federal tax agents estimated Klan membership at not more than 10,000, but the Klan appeared to be making new converts and influencing events.

Dr. Green took pride in his three years of kluxing. At a Konklave in 1949, he was elevated from Grand Dragon to Imperial Wizard, a position that had been vacant since 1944. With the new title went a gold and red robe, a blue cape, and a gold hood with the words "Imperial Wizard" emblazoned on it.

Imperial Wizard Green's moment of glory was short-lived. On August 18, 1949, he dropped dead of a heart attack while tending his flower garden in Atlanta. Green's passage "from the Invisible Empire to the Empire Invisible" marked the beginning of the end for the postwar Klan. In the vacuum created by Green's death, Klandom was once again torn by division and violence, which gave anti-Klan Southerners a chance to strike crushing blows.

Green's successor as Imperial Wizard was Samuel W. Roper. A big, slow-talking man, Roper had been an Atlanta policeman for twenty-five years before taking over as head of the Georgia Bureau of Investigation in the early 1940s. Since 1944, he had worked closely with Dr. Green in the Association of Georgia Klans. Roper was a poor speaker, but his biggest problem was competition from new Klans in the South.

Several sharp promoters hoped they could replace Green in Klandom by creating their own Klans. In Georgia, two of Green's enemies founded the "Original Southern Klans, Inc.," which spread into northern Florida. This group soon collapsed, but the Florida branch was kept alive by Bill Hendrix, a Tallahassee plumbing contractor. Hendrix called his group the "Northern and Southern Knights of the Ku Klux Klan," and he mysteriously announced that the head of the secret order was "Permanent Emperor, Samuel II." Proclaiming a fight against Communism, Hendrix called for a week of cross burnings across the country "to light up the skies of America in protest against Communism." Some observers suggested that Hendrix was more interested in the $16 membership fee than he was in Communism.

Without question the most colorful of the new crop of Klan "leaders" was Dr. Lycurgus Spinks. Sporting shoulder-length white hair, the aging Dr. Spinks was a born showman. According to Ralph McGill of the Atlanta *Constitution*, Spinks picked up the title "doctor" on the lecture circuit. "Doc used to be one of those fellows who lectured on sex, hiring halls and talking to 'men only' and then giving a matinee for 'ladies only.'" Spinks ran for governor of Mississippi in 1947, getting only 4,344 votes out of the approximately 350,000 ballots cast. Hoping to find greener pastures in Klandom, Spinks created the so-called "Knights of the Ku Klux Klan of America" just five days after Dr. Green's death. The self-appointed "Imperial Emperor immediately boasted 265,000 followers in six states. This outrageous claim got Spinks an interview on *Meet the Press*, a national radio program. Spinks soon disappeared from sight, but not before one angry Klan leader guessed that Spinks was Imperial Emperor "over himself and one other guy."

In the absence of strong central leadership, Klansmen ran amok in a wave of terror that spread over the Southeast. Fifty-one incidents of mob violence were recorded in a three-month period during 1949. Many of the victims were whites who ran afoul of some Klan standard of conduct. Klansmen burned a cross in front of a Miami church whose white congregation invited a black minister to preach. A mob of Kluxers beat up two

Chattanooga war veterans who refused to kneel before a burning cross. Georgia Klansmen whipped a man who supposedly had cursed at his mother.

Although the pattern of Klan violence was similar to that of the 1920s, the southern response was not. Newspapermen, civic leaders, clergymen, and politicians openly condemned the Invisible Empire. Even before Imperial Wizard Green passed from the scene, the Klan had come under heavy pressure in the South. Asked why Klansmen wore masks, Green told an interviewer: "So many people are prejudiced against the Klan these days that members are afraid they'll lose their jobs, their influence in public affairs, or otherwise be penalized if they are recognized."

Resistance to the Klan took a variety of forms. When some 300 Klansmen and Klanswomen paraded in West Columbia, South Carolina, college students threw stink bombs and firecrackers at the group. Robed Klansmen in Iron City, Georgia, were peppered with birdshot by angry local citizens. A Klan Klavalcade through Tallahassee, Florida, brought disapproving words from Governor Fuller Warren. "The hooded hoodlums and sheeted jerks who paraded the streets of Tallahassee made a disgusting and alarming spectacle," Warren observed. "These covered cowards who call themselves Klansmen quite obviously have set out to terrorize minority groups in Florida."

Alabama, which had suffered some of the worst Klan violence, led the way in curbing the Klan. The Federated Ku Klux Klans of Alabama, Inc., openly engaged in brutal terrorism during 1949. Marauding Klansmen dragged a terrified Birmingham white woman from her home and forced her to watch as a cross blazed in her front yard. She was accused of "renting rooms" to high school students. Another Birmingham mother was flogged because the Klan did not approve of her daughter's boyfriend. A war veteran was beaten for neglecting his family.

Outraged citizens mobilized to stem this tide of terror. Birmingham newspapers publicized the gruesome details of the Klan's night-riding. The American Legion condemned the mob attacks and offered a $3,000 reward for information leading to the conviction of the masked culprits. A committee of 500, composed of Birmingham's leading citizens, campaigned for punishment of the guilty parties. Governor James E. Folsom told reporters that "mobs, hooded or unhooded, are not going to rule Alabama."

The local prosecutor, himself a former Klansman, launched an investigation that led to the indictment of eighteen Klansmen for mob violence. When the Grand Wizard of the Alabama Klans, William Morris, refused to hand over a list of Klan members to a grand jury, he spent two months in a Birmingham jail for contempt of court. Although the state was unable to convict any Klansmen after a year-long campaign, the legal proceedings scared many Knights into quitting. The wave of violence also came to an end, and Alabama capped its anti-Klan crusade by outlawing the wearing of masks in public.

Across the border in Georgia, the federal government prosecuted twelve Klansmen. The defendants, including a sheriff and three of his deputies, were charged with conspiracy to violate the civil rights of seven blacks who were arrested without cause and then turned over to a mob of Klan floggers. A jury in Rome, Georgia, found the sheriff and one of his deputies guilty.

With the Klan on the defensive, Georgia, South Carolina, and Florida joined Alabama in outlawing the wearing of masks. Over twenty cities, including Atlanta and Miami, also passed antimask measures. Although these laws did not prevent the various Klans from operating, they were symbolic of a new attitude in some areas of the South.

Attempts to get around the law made the Klan look ridiculous. At a rally in Augusta, Georgia, Knights hid behind dark glasses and false mustaches. Some even put on lipstick and rouge to disguise themselves. Instead of striking terror in the hearts of spectators, these foolish-looking Klansmen sparked only laughter.

Reflecting on the dismal state of Klandom in late 1949, former Imperial Wizard Hiram Wesley Evans told a reporter: "You can't start new fire with wet ashes. Under Doctor Green the Klan might have amounted to something, for he was an old Klansman and the old-timers would follow him. Now it's breaking up into little splinter groups that won't last. I'm sorry to see it, but the times and the temper of the people have changed. The Klan can't live without the mask. Unmask it and in two years it will be dead—no more powerful politically than the Red Men."

Two years later the splintered Klan was almost dead. Again, an eruption of mob violence undermined the hooded order. After the outbursts in Alabama and Georgia, the setting for the next wave of violence shifted to North Carolina. There the Associated

Order of Carolina Klans, a creation of Grand Dragon Thomas L. Hamilton, terrorized the citizens of Columbus County, North Carolina, for almost a year. The Invisible Empire arrived in the farming area along the South Carolina border in 1950. Soon Klan rallies attracted as many as 5,000 people from the region. During 1951, night-riding Klansmen kidnapped and flogged at least a dozen people. Most of the victims were whites accused of some immoral deed such as drunkenness, failure to attend church, disrespect toward parents, or simply laziness. Newspaper editors in the Columbus County towns of Tabor City and Whiteville tried to expose the "infamous marauders," but ultimately Klansmen themselves sealed their doom by breaking a federal law against kidnappers who cross state lines.

In 1952, the FBI rounded up ten Klansmen from the Columbus County Klavern and charged them with kidnapping. The group, which included two former police chiefs, was accused of taking a white couple across the state line into South Carolina and whipping them with a machine belt three inches wide and two feet long. The two victims were left with the warning, "Go home, quit drinking and go to church." FBI agents were assisted in their investigation by the local sheriff and his deputies. Reflecting the new attitude toward night-riding Klansmen, one sheriff suggested, "Every time they raise their ugly heads, slap 'em down. They'll learn fast enough that way."

Similar sentiments were expressed by many North Carolinians. Following the lead of local newspaper editors who won Pulitzer prizes for their courageous stands against the Klan, the mayor of Tabor City declared that "Columbus County is just like the rest of the nation, and we feel that there is no place for this outlaw action." Even the man who had served as Grand Dragon of the state's KKK in the 1920s condemned the outrages of the new Klan. "There is no place in North Carolina for the Ku Klux Klan," the former Klansman observed. "If those fellows are guilty, I think they ought to suffer the severe penalty of the law."

Suffer they did. The ten Klansmen arrested by the FBI were found guilty of kidnapping in a federal trial. The judge imposed sentences ranging from probation to five years in jail. State courts mopped up what was left of North Carolina's night riders. Ultimately, over fifty Klansmen were fined and twenty were jailed for their parts in the reign of terror.

Capping the legal assault against the Klan was the guilty plea of Grand Dragon Hamilton, who got four years in the state prison for flogging a black woman. In the wake of Hamilton's conviction a North Carolina newspaper concluded: "The Ku Klux Klan has been kaught, konquered, klobbered, and dekapitated."

Elsewhere, the Invisible Empire had difficulty keeping old members, let alone finding new ones. The leader of the Florida Klan thought violence had harmed the Klan. "All that trouble in North Carolina hurt," he observed. "People want to forget all that beating and bloodiness."

By 1954, the Ku Klux Klan was extinct or dormant in the South, where it had attempted a comeback after World War II. Weak, corrupt, and jealous leaders were unable to win a very large following for the various Klan groups that competed for members. The Klan's record of lawlessness drove out many Knights, and the courts finished off most of what was left. There remained only ragtag bunches of disorganized Klansmen scattered across parts of the South.

9/Kombating Integration

THE ACCELERATION OF THE CIVIL RIGHTS MOVEMENT BROUGHT NEW
life to the Ku Klux Klan. Until the mid-1950s, the southern system of separating blacks
and whites from cradle to grave generally prevailed. Segregated hospitals, schools,
restaurants, rest rooms, churches, and even cemeteries had all been part of the southern
way of life for as long as anyone could remember. Then, in 1954, the U.S. Supreme Court
ruled that separate schools were inherently unequal and, therefore, violated constitutional guarantees of equal protection for all citizens. The following year, the Court ruled
that public schools should be integrated "with all deliberate speed," but this decision
encouraged the southern states to act with greater deliberation than speed. Meanwhile,
white Southerners began to dig in their heels to resist racial integration. Klansmen
quickly became the most violent opponents of school integration.

Beginning with the 1956 school year, Klansmen rallied across the Deep South to
protest against desegregation. Some 200 Florida Knights attracted 1,000 spectators to a
cow pasture near Lakeland for a cross burning and fiery speech making. Hooded speakers
promised that the races "shall not be mixed in the public schools of Florida," because
"God never did intend for us to integrate with Negroes." Similar rallies were held by
various Klan groups in South Carolina and Alabama. White-robed speakers routinely
condemned the Supreme Court and integration. One of the largest Klan rallies since

World War II drew over 3,500 Knights and their families to the birthplace of the twentieth-century Klan at Stone Mountain.

Ever ready to make a buck off the fears of white Protestants, ambitious Kluxers created a number of new Klans to channel funds into their own pockets. By far, the largest of the new groups was the "U. S. Klans, Knights of the Ku Klux Klan," incorporated in Georgia in 1955 by Eldon Lee Edwards. A tough-talking paint sprayer at an Atlanta auto plant, Edwards proclaimed himself Imperial Wizard and took over what was left of the old Association of Georgia Klans. Promising to maintain "segregated schools at any and all costs," Edwards signed up recruits for his U.S. Klans in Georgia and neighboring states, particularly Alabama and South Carolina. Integration was the main concern, but Kluxers managed to connect other longtime foes to a supposedly giant conspiracy to break down segregation.

"The niggers are the main thing with us now," Louisiana's Grand Dragon of the U.S. Klans observed. "We are not fighting Jews and Catholics except where they help the niggers."

"I ain't got nothin' against niggers," the Grand Dragon of South Carolina declared. "I don't believe most of them would be causing any trouble if it wasn't for the NAACP [National Association for the Advancement of Colored People] and the Jews. I understand there are a lot of Communists trying to get us to integrate with the niggers so we'll breed down the race."

In addition to Edwards' U.S. Klans, over twenty other Klan groups sprang up to exploit racial fears. In South Carolina, a prospective Klansman could join any number of different orders, including the "Association of South Carolina Klans," "National Ku Klux Klan," "South Carolina Knights of the Ku Klux Klan," "Independent Knights of the Ku Klux Klan," and the "Palmetto Knights of the Ku Klux Klan." Other small Klan groups operated in North Carolina, Mississippi, Louisiana, Arkansas, and Texas. Many of the competing groups were offshoots of the U.S. Klans. In Alabama, dissenters formed the "Gulf Ku Klux Klan." Knights of the Chattanooga Klavern of the U.S. Klans seceded and created the "Dixie Klans, Knights of the Ku Klux Klan." Reflecting on Klan operations in the 1950s, Bill Hendrix of the Florida Knights of the Ku Klux Klan later described the

Invisible Empire as "a conglomeration of different organizations breaking up, going together, and not getting along."

Membership in most of these independent Klans was small. Although the exact figures are unknown, only the U.S. Klans, with 12,000 to 15,000 Knights, had a sizable following. Most of the competing Klans had well under 1,500 members at their peak in the 1950s.

Because of its previous record for lawlessness, the Invisible Empire attracted only the most desperate element of Southern society. Day laborers and poor whites generally made up the bulk of Klan members. More prosperous whites who wanted to fight integration joined the White Citizens' Councils that spread across the South during the 1950s. Some 300,000 middle-class Southerners, including businessmen and politicians, flocked into the White Citizens' Councils to defend white supremacy. Unlike the Klan, the Citizens' Councils operated openly and publicly emphasized nonviolence in the bitter battle against integration.

Long a breeder of violence, the Invisible Empire attracted racists who took the law into their hands. A 1959 study reported 530 cases of racial violence and intimidation in the South during the four years after the Supreme Court ordered integration of public schools. In addition to cross burnings, beatings, floggings, and shootings, the acts of lawlessness included a new twist—the bombing of schools, homes, and churches. Some 140 dynamite explosions ripped the South during the reign of terror between 1956 and 1963. Since most of the racial crimes went unsolved, it will never be known how many involved Klansmen. However, in a few notable cases, the Ku Klux Klan was directly linked to the wave of antiblack violence.

Montgomery, Alabama, dramatically fueled the embers of the southern civil rights movement. In late 1955, a tired black woman, Rosa Parks, sparked the protest movement when she refused to give up her seat to a white person on a crowded city bus. Mrs. Parks' subsequent arrest for violating the local bus segregation law led to a complete black boycott of the bus system. The leader of the nonviolent protest to force integration of Montgomery's buses was a twenty-six-year-old minister, Martin Luther King, Jr., who soon emerged as the leader of the civil rights movement. The first major victory in the budding movement came in Montgomery when a year-long campaign resulted in a federal court order requiring integration of the city's buses.

In the wake of King's first victory, violence erupted in Montgomery. During the month following the court-ordered integration, bombers dynamited four black churches and the homes of three boycott leaders, including that of King. Miraculously, no one was injured in the blasts. A police investigation led Montgomery's police chief to conclude that "these bombings were perpetrated by members of the Montgomery branch of the Ku Klux Klan." Several Knights of the U.S. Klans were among those later accused of committing the bombing attacks, but the charges were dropped after a jury acquitted two of the defendants.

Elsewhere in Alabama, six Klansmen were found guilty of sadistically mutilating a black man in Birmingham. The man had been kidnapped at random following a Klan meeting and tortured in order to "test the worthiness" of a Klansman up for promotion in Klan ranks.

Several other communities also cracked down on Klan violence. In Greenville, South Carolina, four Klansmen received prison terms of one to six years for beating a black man who was taking care of a family of white children. A Charlotte, North Carolina, jury convicted three members of a splinter group, the National Christian Knights of the Ku Klux Klan, on charges of plotting to bomb a black church.

These few cases where Klansmen were punished for acts of terrorism undoubtedly revealed only the tip of the iceberg. Untried in courtrooms were dozens of other Klansmen who also resorted to violence during the 1950s.

In one well-publicized case, victims of the Klan decided to fight fire with fire. North Carolina's system of racial segregation extended to Indians who were kept separate from both whites and blacks. In 1958 in Robeson County, which was almost equally divided among whites, Indians, and blacks, the Klan tried to frighten some Lumbee Indians. A cross was burned in the yard of an Indian family in a white neighborhood, and another at the home of an Indian woman accused of dating a white man. When a small group of Klansmen led by Grand Wizard James W. "Catfish" Cole then tried to hold a rally in Robeson County, they found themselves surrounded by angry and armed Lumbee Indians. As the Knights started their ceremony, the Indians attacked, firing at the group. After a brief exchange of gunfire in which no one was seriously injured, the Indians held the field and captured Klan equipment including a KKK banner. To add insult to injury,

Grand Wizard Cole was found guilty of inciting a riot and sentenced to two years in jail.

The 1950s ended with the splintered Klan increasingly identified as a bunch of terrorists. Although they found little public support in the South, Klansmen continued to get away with most of their acts of violence against blacks and other supporters of civil rights.

The Klan's unpopularity and record of lawlessness drove Bill Hendrix to retire as longtime leader of one of Florida's Klan groups. Explaining his reasons for quitting, Hendrix said, "I cannot agree to go outside the law to maintain segregation."

The year 1960 marked a new stage in the civil rights movement and the counteroffensive of the Invisible Empire. In February, 1960, four black college students sat down at a lunch counter "for whites only" in Greensboro, North Carolina. When the blacks were not served, they remained seated in protest until closing time. They kept returning with each new day, thereby effectively shutting down the Woolworth lunch counter and disrupting business in the store. The Greensboro "sit-in" demonstration continued until Woolworths gave in and integrated its facilities. Blacks around the South quickly adopted the successful sit-in technique. Within the next eighteen months, 70,000 persons participated in sit-ins across the South that desegregated eating places in over 100 communities.

Klansmen immediately mobilized to rebuff the rash of civil rights demonstrations. However, Kluxers were hampered by the courage of the young blacks, who did not frighten easily. Furthermore, extensive TV and newspaper coverage made it difficult for Klansmen to use traditional strong-arm methods. Knights were reduced to burning crosses to show, in the words of one member, "we are organized and are ready for business." Robed and hooded Klansmen also held demonstrations in several cities, but their presence only increased the likelihood that no one would enter a store with civil rights workers inside and Klansmen outside. Apparently frustrated by their inability to stop the sit-ins, several whites seized a black man in Houston and carved the initials "KKK" in his chest.

As the civil rights movement gained momentum, competing Klans jockeyed to take advantage of white fears. Of the more than twenty Klan groups that operated in the 1950s, less than ten survived into the 1960s. The largest was Georgia's U.S. Klans, Knights of the

Ku Klux Klan, Inc., but it broke apart after the sudden death of Imperial Wizard Eldon Lee Edwards in 1960. Robert "Wild Bill" Davidson was elected to succeed the fallen Edwards, but Edwards' widow resisted the move. This internal dissension soon led to Davidson's resignation and his creation of a rival group, known as the "United Klans of America, Knights of the Ku Klux Klan, Inc." So many Georgia Knights deserted the old U.S. Klans that by the mid-1960s its membership was confined to a single Klavern in Atlanta.

The new United Klans of America quickly overshadowed all other groups in the Invisible Empire. This growth was largely due to the leadership of Robert Shelton, a thirty-year-old former rubber plant worker from Tuscaloosa, Alabama. The thin, craggy-faced Shelton had been Alabama's Grand Dragon of the U.S. Klans until expelled by Imperial Wizard Edwards in 1957. In typical Klan fashion, Shelton had then formed his own group in Alabama, and in 1961 he merged with the new United Klans of America (UKA). He soon became Imperial Wizard of the UKA, which was based largely in Georgia and Alabama at the time.

Imperial Wizard Shelton pitched his appeal to whites fearful of civil rights, or "civil wrongs" as he preferred to say. "The 'civil wrongs' campaign and the attacks Northerners are making on Southern people are driving a deep wedge between black and white," Shelton told audiences. Although he presented the United Klans of America as a "new, modern, jet-age Klan," Shelton admitted that the ideals "have not changed one bit since 1867." In defense of white supremacy, Shelton attacked not only blacks but also Jews and Communists, who, he claimed, were behind the civil rights movement.

"We are one Klan in our unchangeable determination that these United States will be saved from destruction under this foul combination of Negro-Jewish communism," Imperial Wizard Shelton told a North Carolina audience. "Yes, our mortal enemy as of old is the jungle descendant of the Negro, but today he has banded together with the non-white, money-drunk, anti-Christian Jew who has influenced him, financed him, propagandized him, defended him falsely in our courts and enslaved him into his Jewish-owned and controlled National Association for the Advancement of Colored People."

Explaining the aims of the United Klan of America, Shelton made "an open declaration of war against the evils of Negroism and Jewism and the Jewish Communists." The Klan, he said, would "take back this country from alien thieves and traitors." Shelton expressed conflicting views on the means his Klan would use. On the one hand, he disavowed violence. "It is a legal war, a peaceful war, a constitutional war—a war of ballots, not bullets." On the other hand, he left open the possibility that Klansmen would take the law into their own hands. "Our weapons are ballots not bullets, but we will defend ourselves, our homes, our loved ones. We will never night ride again, *unless* we are forced to defend our homes."

At a Georgia rally, the fire-eating Imperial Wizard was more blunt. "We don't want no violence, but we ain't gonna let the niggers spit in our face either," Shelton told 4,000 spectators. "I'm afraid," he concluded, "that before this [civil rights] movement is brought to defeat, there will be more bloodshed."

In his early days, Robert Shelton himself was scarcely a model of peacefulness. He openly opposed an Alabama law that would have made flogging by night riders a capital offense. Although paying lip service to law and order, Shelton said he was "glad that there are still men somewhere who will take matters in their own hands when the hands of the law are tied."

Shelton's involvement in violence against civil rights demonstrators brought him to the attention of the federal courts. In the spring of 1961, civil rights workers challenged the southern practice of segregation on buses and in bus stations that catered to interstate passengers. To bring attention to this situation that the courts had declared unconstitutional, blacks and whites boarded integrated buses in the North and rode into the Deep South. Although the law was on their side, the so-called "freedom riders" were assaulted and badly beaten by Alabama mobs that included Klansmen. One freedom rider required some fifty stitches to close his wounds. A federal judge in Alabama blamed Klansmen for the mob violence, and he named Robert Shelton as one of those responsible. The judge ordered Shelton and other Klansmen to stop interfering with bus passengers. Federal marshals were sent in to uphold the court order and protect freedom riders. As a result, another segregationist barrier fell.

The successful campaign of freedom riders showed how Klan terrorism was self-defeating. The beating of nonviolent freedom riders and the burning of buses generated widespread sympathy for civil rights among Americans in the North and West who watched indignantly as violence flashed across their TV screens. Public opinion outside the South supported the federal intervention that ultimately spelled the end of segregated buses. As in other cases, antiblack violence inspired by the Klan contributed to the very changes so hated by Klansmen.

Nevertheless, the Klan's violent crusade against integration continued. When a riot greeted the first blacks to attend the University of Georgia in 1962, eight of the nine men arrested were admitted Klansmen. On a Sunday morning in 1963, a bomb blast rocked a black church in Birmingham, Alabama, and four young girls died in the explosion. Fourteen years later, local officials charged a former Klansman with setting the bomb, and a Birmingham jury found him guilty.

Imperial Wizard Shelton tried unsuccessfully to change the Klan's image by appearing in a coat and tie and downplaying violent methods, but even he could not get away from rhetoric endorsing mob action: "I do not advocate violence," Shelton told a Mississippi audience, "but if you have to resort to it after all else fails, then use it." Other Klan leaders echoed the same line. "The antidote for poison is poison," declared Georgia's Grand Dragon. "I do not believe in violence, but I do believe in self-preservation. This has always been a fighting organization—you can check on the history of the Klan."

The Klan's history of violence limited its appeal to a tiny minority of Southerners in the 1960s. Imperial Wizard Shelton brought new members and a degree of unity to the Invisible Empire, but his following remained relatively small. Under Shelton's leadership, the United Klans of America spread across the South and became the most powerful group in Klandom with an estimated 15,000 members in the mid-1960s. The dozen or so other Klan organizations had a combined total of less than 2,000 members with no more than 400 Knights in any one group. Although Klansmen could be found all over the South, the heart of Klan strength was in the southeastern states of Georgia, Alabama, South Carolina, and Florida. Even in those states, the Invisible Empire had no political power. Too weak to influence politics, the Ku Klux Klan became the last refuge of extreme racists prone to violence.

10 / Ku Klux Killers

AFTER YEARS OF GAINING MOMENTUM, THE CIVIL RIGHTS BANDWAGON rolled headlong across the South in 1963. During one three-month period, civil rights workers held 1,412 separate demonstrations in southern cities. White Southerners intent on preventing change resorted to the usual array of tactics, including everything from arrests to beatings and killings. Under mounting pressure, President John F. Kennedy finally called on Congress to pass legislation guaranteeing blacks the right to vote and equal access to schools and public facilities like restaurants. The bill he proposed in the summer of 1963 promised better federal protection of the rights sought by blacks.

As the civil rights movement spread like wildfire, its supporters prepared the first large-scale assault on the racial barriers of Mississippi, the one southern state that had escaped any large demonstrations. Secure behind the so-called "Magnolia Curtain," many white Mississippians saw their state as the last bastion of white supremacy. This attitude led in 1963 to the assassination of Medgar Evers, the state director of the National Association for the Advancement of Colored People and one of the first local blacks to work for equal rights. When a white man was tried in 1964 for killing Evers, the governor of Mississippi, Ross Barnett, made a point of stopping by the trial to talk with the defendant. The all-white jury failed to convict the accused murderer.

The campaign against discrimination in Mississippi was organized by the Council of

Federated Organizations (COFO), a coalition of civil rights groups. COFO had begun sending a few workers into the Magnolia State in 1962, but they had made little progress in the effort to get blacks registered to vote. Blatant discrimination and terrorism stood in the way of blacks who wanted to vote. On one occasion, night riders ambushed several COFO workers, one of whom was badly wounded. By 1964, COFO had established a beachhead in Mississippi, but the campaign had bogged down. The decision was made to bring in hundred of reinforcements for a peaceful, nonviolent offensive during the summer of 1964. The new recruits for the Mississippi Summer Project were to be young volunteers, primarily college students from outside the South. Under the command of COFO, they were to spend their summer vacations working on voter education projects and helping blacks to register.

As civil rights workers mobilized for the Summer Project, so too did local Klansmen. The Klan had been scarcely visible in Mississippi until some fearful, bitter-end segregationists turned to it to fight COFO activities. In 1963, a small group of Mississippians joined the Original Knights of the Ku Klux Klan of Louisiana, and later that year they broke away to form the White Knights of the Ku Klux Klan of Mississippi, which became one of the most violent Klan groups in history. The founder and self-styled Imperial Wizard of Mississippi's White Knights was Sam Bowers, Jr., a thirty-nine-year-old businessman from Laurel. Some 2,000 Mississippians enlisted in the White Knights' crusade to repel the invasion of COFO workers planned for late June, 1964. On joining the White Knights, new members swore to "embrace the Spirit of Christian militancy" and if necessary to "die in order to preserve Christian Civilization." In fiery orations, Imperial Wizard Bowers encouraged Klansmen to prepare for the coming battle.

"We must use all of the time which is left to us preparing to meet this attack," he secretly told his followers. "Weapons and ammunition must be accumulated and stored; squads must drill; propaganda equipment must be set up ready to roll; counterattack maps, plans and information must be studied and learned."

Clearly approving violence and disregarding the law, Bowers ordered White Knights to stay out of trouble "until you can catch [COFO workers] outside the law, then under Mississippi law you have a right to kill them."

The secret order of White Knights announced its presence through a series of cross burnings during the spring of 1964. However, the Mississippi Klan was ready to go beyond nonviolent intimidation of blacks and civil rights workers. "The issue," a Klan poster declared, "is clearly one of personal, physical SELF-DEFENSE OR DEATH for the American Anglo-Saxons."

For the Klan, a symbol of all it hated was Michael Schwerner, a twenty-four-year-old bearded Jewish New Yorker. Early in 1964, Schwerner and his wife, Rita, arrived in the eastern Mississippi city of Meridian. As low-paid employees of the Congress of Racial Equality (CORE), the Schwerners were in the vanguard of the COFO force that would descend on Mississippi some six months later. The couple set up offices in downtown Meridian. From there Michael Schwerner moved out to make contacts among blacks in the surrounding area.

To help pave his way among suspicious blacks, Schwerner relied heavily on James Chaney, a twenty-year-old black who had grown up in Meridian. Traveling in a 1963 blue Ford station wagon, the black and white pair became unmistakable companions in an area where the two races rarely mingled on a basis of equality.

Both Michael Schwerner's background and his civil rights activities immediately made him an object of extreme hatred among local whites. He became widely known as "the atheist Jew," or simply as "Jew-boy." Harassment of the COFO workers took several forms. Threatening and vile telephone calls plagued the Schwerners. The anonymous callers warned, "Get out of town, you damn Communists, or you'll get it!" Sometimes the message was just a string of obscenities from some woman who presumably was a God-fearing, white Christian.

Undaunted, the Schwerners stepped up their activities. In May, Michael organized a black boycott of several Meridian stores that refused to hire black clerks even though they catered to black customers. Picketing the stores led to Schwerner's arrest for blocking the sidewalk. He pleaded guilty and paid a small fine.

At about the same time, Schwerner was marked for "extermination" by the White Knights of the Ku Klux Klan. The self-appointed executioners awaited only the opportunity to seize their victim.

On Saturday, June 20, 1964, Congress passed the civil rights bill proposed by President Kennedy before his assassination. Late that evening, Michael Schwerner returned to Meridian with Andrew Goodman, one of the first COFO volunteers to arrive in Mississippi for the Summer Project. Goodman, a white college student also from New York City, was deeply committed to the cause of civil rights.

On Sunday, June 21, his first full day in Mississippi, Goodman went with Schwerner and Chaney to investigate the burning of a black church in neighboring Neshoba County. White Knights had attacked the church the week before, apparently expecting to find their intended victim, Michael Schwerner. In their frustration, the Klansmen had also badly beaten several blacks whom they had found there. The assault brought the Klan's primary target, Schwerner, and his two companions to the church.

After visiting the burned-out church and talking with some of the congregation members, the conspicuous trio headed toward the city of Philadelphia, seat of Neshoba County. Chaney was driving the blue station wagon, with Schwerner and Goodman alongside him on the front seat. Before arriving in Philadelphia, the three were stopped by the Neshoba County deputy sheriff, Cecil Price. Price later claimed that he stopped the car on a speeding violation, although two state troopers who observed the car said it was not going over the speed limit. Nevertheless, Deputy Sheriff Price arrested Chaney for speeding and held Schwerner and Goodman for "investigation." Accompanied by the two state troopers, he booked the three civil rights workers into Philadelphia's county jail about 4:15 in the afternoon. Schwerner asked permission to make a phone call, knowing COFO workers in Meridian would be worried if the trio did not return to headquarters by 4 o'clock as planned. Price would not allow a phone call.

Within an hour after the jailing of Chaney, Goodman, and Schwerner, anxious COFO workers had routinely contacted local and state authorities. However, calls to the Neshoba county jail, the sheriff's office, and the state police brought denials that any officials knew the whereabouts of the civil rights workers. The three undoubtedly felt safe while in jail, but they could not have been more wrong. The Klan's opportunity to eliminate Michael Schwerner was at hand.

By 10 o'clock in the evening, the Klan conspirators had gathered. They came from the

101

Meridian and Philadelphia areas and waited alongside the highway that linked the two cities. According to the plot, the victims would soon be delivered into the hands of the Klan.

At about 10:30 P.M., Schwerner, Chaney, and Goodman were released from the county jail after posting a $20 cash bond. They got into the blue station wagon and headed south toward Meridian. The trio passed the waiting Klansmen, who joined in pursuit and forced the civil rights workers to stop on a deserted side road.

The Klansmen pulled Schwerner from the station wagon, and one of the White Knights shot him through the heart. Goodman was next, and a single bullet through the heart killed him, too. Chaney apparently struggled, but three shots snuffed out his life. The murderers took the three victims to a burial site about fifteen miles away. The prearranged grave was an earthen dam under construction on a farm outside Philadelphia. The bodies were thrown in a ditch at the foot of the dam and covered with several feet of dirt. In the following weeks, construction workers finished the twenty-foot high dam without knowing that three men lay buried beneath it. After concealing the bodies, the Klansmen took the victims' car to a spot some twenty miles away on the other side of Philadelphia. There they burned the station wagon in hopes of fooling investigators into thinking the bodies were buried in a nearby swamp.

The Klan terrorists completed their deadly mission by dawn. They undoubtedly felt they had struck a blow for white supremacy. However, their cowardly murder of three defenseless young men soon brought disgrace on Mississippi and a federal crackdown on the Klan.

The day after the disappearance of the three civil rights workers, the Federal Bureau of Investigation entered the case. Operating as though it were an ordinary kidnapping, the FBI brought in a task force of agents to follow leads. By the time the bodies would be located, some 150 agents would be working on the Mississippi case. Within two days after the civil rights workers disappeared, their burned-out station wagon was discovered, but an intensive search of the surrounding area failed to turn up any sign of the victims. The Klan had apparently succeeded in throwing the FBI off the track.

As the summer wore on with no break in the case, Klansmen continued terrorizing central Mississippi. During June and July, sixteen black churches were burned to the ground. Fire bombs and gun blasts tore through the homes of blacks involved in the civil rights movement. Burning crosses were a constant reminder of who was behind the violence.

Finally, in August, came the long-awaited break in the case of the three missing civil rights workers. An informer told FBI agents where the bodies could be found.

Forty-four days after their disappearance, a careful search of the new dam turned up the grisly proof that the three young men had been murdered. Until the bodies were found, some white Mississippians had preferred to believe that the incident was a hoax designed to get free publicity for the civil rights movement. The Klan obviously encouraged such speculation, but after discovery of the dead bodies, Klansmen expressed satisfaction.

"This is the first time in history that Christians have carried out the execution of a Jew," Imperial Wizard Bowers gloated.

A Klan newspaper condemned the victims in an apparent attempt to justify the crime. "Schwerner, Chaney and Goodman are not civil-rights workers," the Mississippi Klan argued. "They were Communist Revolutionaries, actively working to undermine and destroy Christian Civilization." The Klan suggested that two possible groups could have committed the murders: "(1) American Patriots who are determined to resist Communism by every available means, and (2) The Communists themselves who will always sacrifice their own members in order to achieve a propaganda victory."

Most people suspected that the Ku Klux Klan was responsible for the deaths, but proving it was difficult. The FBI, under orders from President Lyndon B. Johnson, went to considerable lengths to solve the case and end the terrorism that continued to plague Mississippi. Relying largely on paid informants within the ranks of the White Knights, the FBI gradually began to put its case together. By December, 1964, the federal government felt it had enough evidence for indictments. However, the suspects were not charged with murder, because that is a state crime and Mississippi shared little interest in pressing the case. Washington authorities charged all the suspects with the federal crime of interfering with federally guaranteed civil rights of the three victims.

On December 3, 1964, the FBI arrested twenty-one men associated with the White Knights in the Meridian and Philadelphia areas. Nineteen, including the Neshoba County sheriff and Deputy Sheriff Cecil Price, were charged with conspiring to interfere with the rights of Schwerner, Chaney, and Goodman by killing them. Price was charged with setting the plot in motion by arresting the three civil rights workers without lawful cause and then joining the others to intercept the victims after their release from jail.

The legal proceedings that followed were complex and drawn out. Not until October, 1967, over three years after the murders, did anyone go to trial. By that time, there were eighteen defendants charged with conspiring to murder Schwerner, Chaney, and Goodman. Among them were Imperial Wizard Sam Bowers, Neshoba County Sheriff Lawrence Rainey and Deputy Sheriff Cecil Price. The government's case was based largely on the testimony of two former White Knights, one of whom admitted participating in the murder conspiracy. This witness told the court how Klansmen had gathered in Meridian on the fateful Sunday afternoon in June, 1964. They then went to the spot south of Philadelphia where they waited for the three victims to pass after their release from jail. According to this testimony, Deputy Sheriff Price led the chase of the blue station wagon, and he forced the three civil rights workers to a stop by flashing the red light on his patrol car. After that, the fatal shots were fired.

Defense attorneys presented witnesses who swore the defendants were elsewhere at the time of the murders. The defense also tried to prove that the Klansmen were men of good character. Throughout the week-long trial, the accused appeared relaxed, often breaking into laughter, apparently confident that no all-white Mississippi jury would convict Klansmen of anything related to the murder of civil rights workers.

To the surprise of many, the federal jury found seven of the eighteen defendants guilty. The seven, including Sam Bowers and Cecil Price, were sentenced to federal prison for terms ranging from three to ten years. Imperial Wizard Bowers received a ten-year term, which was the maximum possible under the federal law. All seven appealed their convictions, but higher courts refused to reverse the guilty findings. In 1970, they began serving their sentences.

Although the conviction of the Klansmen spelled the end of the White Knights, the

104

Klan's reign of terror in Mississippi had continued during the years of legal battles. In January, 1966, Klansmen decided to put an end to the activities of Vernon Dahmer, a black farmer who ran a grocery store in a small town near Hattiesburg in southeastern Mississippi. Dahmer headed the local chapter of the NAACP, and he led a campaign to help register black voters. One night, two carloads of Klansmen drove into Dahmer's front yard. While several White Knights fired shotgun blasts into the house, others hurled fire bombs. Dahmer died in the flames.

FBI agents found a mass of incriminating evidence at Dahmer's home, including a gun one of the Klan terrorists had dropped. Several informants within the Klan provided the FBI with a list of suspects, led by Imperial Wizard Sam Bowers. Within three months, the federal government officially charged Bowers and thirteen other Klansmen with conspiring to injure, oppress, and threaten Vernon Dahmer in the free exercise of his constitutional rights. The state of Mississippi later filed arson and murder charges against many of the Klansmen implicated by the FBI. Ultimately, the testimony of one of the terrorists who pleaded guilty sent five other White Knights to jail for terms ranging from ten years to life imprisonment. In this case, deadlocked juries failed twice to convict Sam Bowers, who nevertheless served time for his part in the murders of Schwerner, Chaney, and Goodman.

The last gasp of Klan violence in eastern Mississippi came in 1968. For several months Klan terrorists turned their attention to Jews living in Jackson and Meridian. Dynamite blasts first ripped apart a Jackson synagogue and the home of its rabbi. Then a bomb destroyed part of a synagogue in Meridian. After that, the FBI learned from informants that the next Klan target would be a prominent Meridian Jewish leader. On the basis of this information, Meridian police laid a trap for the bombers. In the resulting shoot-out, a Klanswoman was killed. Her partner survived only to be sentenced to prison for thirty years. As a result of the concerted effort by the federal government and the state, the wave of Klan terror came to an end in Mississippi by 1969.

Similar outbursts of Klan violence also plagued neighboring states during the 1960s. The terror was not only senseless but also often arbitrary. In 1964, Lt. Colonel Lemuel A. Penn, a black educator in the army reserve, was driving home from summer training when he was killed by a shotgun blast from a passing car on a Georgia highway. Within days, the FBI identified three men as prime suspects in the apparently random murder of Penn. All three were members of the United Klans of America. Despite incriminating testimony from one of the Klansmen, a Georgia jury found the two alleged triggermen not guilty of murder. However, a federal jury found the two men guilty of conspiring to interfere with Penn's constitutional rights by killing him. The two Klansmen drew ten-year prison terms.

The murder of whites, especially northern whites, generated much greater national attention. In 1965, the ambush killing of Viola Liuzzo led to a sweeping federal investigation of the Klan. Mrs. Liuzzo, a Detroit housewife and mother of five children, was in Alabama for one of the largest civil rights demonstrations in history. The protest—a march from Selma to Montgomery—was in response to police brutality in restricting a voter registration drive in Selma. Thousands of white Northerners, including Mrs. Liuzzo, swelled the ranks of local blacks to form a demonstration that numbered some 12,000 people when it reached the state capital of Montgomery on March 25, 1965. After the rally Mrs. Liuzzo helped drive demonstrators back to Selma. As she returned to Montgomery in the company of a young black man, a car passed hers and someone fired a pistol shot that killed her instantly.

Within hours, an FBI informant told agents he was with three fellow Klansmen when they committed the murder. This information led to the immediate arrest and subsequent conviction of the three Klansmen on the federal charge of conspiring to deprive Mrs. Liuzzo of her constitutional rights. The three received the maximum ten-year prison sentences for the crime.

The senseless killing of Mrs. Liuzzo brought more federal pressure on the Klan. The day after her murder, President Lyndon B. Johnson dramatically went before a national TV audience to announce the FBI arrests of four Klan suspects. The angry president charged that Mrs. Liuzzo "was murdered by the enemies of justice who for decades have used the rope and the gun and the tar and the feathers to terrorize their neighbors." Himself a Southerner, Johnson blasted the Klan as "a hooded society of bigots." He warned members "to get out of the Ku Klux Klan now and return to decent society before it is too late." Finally, the president called for a congressional investigation of the Invisible Empire.

Responding to the president's attack, Imperial Wizard Robert Shelton denounced Johnson as "a damn liar." The leader of the United Klans of America claimed his organization had "never used tar and feathers and a rope." Shelton dismissed the murder of civil rights workers as part of a "trumped-up Communist plot to destroy the right wing in America."

If there was a plot to destroy the Klan, the federal government was leading it. Following Johnson's suggestion, Congress undertook a year-long investigation of the group in 1965. The task was assigned to the House Committee on Un-American Activities (HUAC), which had spent most of the past twenty-five years looking into left-wing groups like the Communist party. Despite HUAC's anti-Communist record, Imperial Wizard Shelton branded the inquiry part of a Communist conspiracy against the Klan.

HUAC's probe was clearly designed to discredit Klan leaders and create dissension in the Klan's ranks. Almost 200 witnesses were questioned by congressmen in public hearings, but most of the Klansmen refused to violate their oath "to die rather than divulge" information about the secret order. When questioned about KKK activities, reluctant witnesses simply stood on their constitutional right, under the Fifth Amendment, not to incriminate themselves. Yet the refusal to testify obviously put Klansmen in a bad light. The embarrassing questions that went unanswered included several related to the handling of Klan finances. The Cadillacs and diamond rings sported by Klan leaders went unexplained. This led one disillusioned Klabee (treasurer) to resign his office while testifying before the committee. Explaining his sudden decision, the former Klansman said, "Anyone who takes the Fifth Amendment either has something to hide or is a Communist."

The House Committee on Un-American Activities turned up little new information about the Invisible Empire. Financial irregularities were an old story. Furthermore, it came as no surprise that the Klan relied on terror. Despite Klan denials of any violent intent, the committee declared that "Klans and their leaders actually incite disrespect for the law and encourage acts of violence." Although dominated by southern congressmen, the committee concluded that "a Klansman does not represent the average citizen of an American community but a community's lowest common denominator."

The impact of HUAC's probe of the Klan is difficult to measure. No anti-Klan legislation resulted from the inquiry. As so often had happened in the past, publicity about the Klan may have attracted as many members as it turned away. The seventeen separate Klans apparently suffered some decline in membership during the HUAC hearings, but the brief downturn was followed by an upswing. The most important result of the congressional hearings was the jailing of Imperial Wizard Robert Shelton and two of his Grand Dragons. In federal court trials, the three were found guilty of contempt of Congress for refusing to turn over Klan records subpoenaed by HUAC. All three received the maximum one-year prison sentence, which was considered unusually stiff. Imperial Wizard Shelton denounced his trial as a "kangaroo court" because the Washington, D.C., jury was made up of three blacks and eight federal employees. However, in the wake of his conviction, Shelton was re-elected Imperial Wizard of the United Klans of America.

While Congress and the courts hounded the Klan in the 1960s, the Federal Bureau of Investigation carried out a secret campaign to disrupt the hooded society. The FBI's "counterintelligence program" (COINTELPRO) was directed at a variety of extremist groups, but in its enthusiasm the FBI apparently resorted to some illegal tactics, such as breaking and entering into private homes. In effect, the federal government used vigilante methods by taking the law into its own hands. The recent discovery of such practices has led to the indictment of several former FBI officials for breaking the law.

The FBI secretly used a number of "dirty tricks" to create dissension among Klansmen and their families. FBI agents sent anonymous postcards to Klansmen with the message: "Trying to hide behind your sheet? You received this. Someone knows who you are." Another postcard with a cartoon of two Klansmen drinking at a bar posed the question, "Which Klan leaders are spending your money tonight?" Other notes falsely accused Klansmen of being FBI informants. The FBI also circulated a phony picture of a Klan leader standing beside Cuba's Communist leader, Fidel Castro. Wives of Klansmen received letters asking, "How come your husband wasn't at Saturday night's Klan meeting? Where was he?" When Klansmen tried to hold a meeting in North Carolina, the FBI called and cancelled all the motel reservations. While serving his prison term for contempt of Congress, Imperial Wizard Shelton received a fake letter supposedly from a Klansman warning, "It hurts me to realize that while you are being held in prison the men you placed in charge are ruining our organization." Unknown to Shelton at the time, the FBI had sent the letter. Since then, revelations of these activities have led Shelton to file several federal law suits against the FBI for alleged damages.

Under increasing pressure from the federal government, the Klan went into a period of decline starting in the late 1960s. Close observers agree that the various Klan groups reached their peak in 1967. Estimates of the total membership spread among some fifteen separate Klans ranged from the FBI figure of 16,000 to a count of 55,000 by the Anti-Defamation League of B'nai B'rith. The largest single group was still Robert Shelton's United Klans of America. Whatever the exact number of Klansmen, they were largely confined to the South and represented a tiny percentage of the population. Moreover, KKK membership began to fall off sharply after 1967 with a number of Klansmen under indictment or on their way to jail for a variety of crimes. Yet the Klan remained alive to haunt the present.

11 / The Klan Today

THE FORTUNES OF THE KU KLUX KLAN RUN IN CYCLES. SINCE ITS founding in 1866, it has gone through three periods of growth followed by years of decline. But like a weed that refuses to die, it has always blossomed after appearing to wither. Its famous history of hate and violence, often justified by myths about defending a way of life, gives it a natural appeal in a country like the United States that is so frequently torn by racial and religious hatreds. The Klan's white robes and hoods have provided a cover for frightened Americans who are willing to break the law in the desperate attempt to prevent unwanted social changes. Yet the Klan's violent methods have finally proved self-defeating.

In the early 1970s, the Ku Klux Klan all but disappeared. Racked by internal bickering, prison terms, and pressure from the FBI, the KKK faced an uncertain future. Furthermore, the victories of the civil rights movement had undermined much of the Klan's appeal. By 1970, federal enforcement of new civil rights laws had made integration and black voting an established fact in the South. Few Southerners any longer thought the clock could be turned back to the days of white supremacy. However, new problems arose to excite old hatreds, and Klan leaders regrouped to protect their interest in hooded bigotry.

When Imperial Wizard Robert Shelton emerged from federal prison in late 1969, he

110

found his empire a shambles. Of the more than 14,000 members of the United Klans of America in the peak years of the 1960s, only about 5,000 remained, according to the FBI. Some Knights had given up their sheets, while others had quit the United Klans of America to form competing Klans. One group of rebels publicly burned their UKA membership cards to show their dissatisfaction with Shelton's leadership. For those who still wanted to wear their sheets and hoods, there were at least a dozen other Klan organizations to choose from, but all were much smaller than the UKA.

In addition to their other worries, Klansmen were suspicious of each other. The FBI's infiltration of the secret order had been so successful that Klansmen hesitated to trust anyone. In desperation the UKA purchased a bunch of lie detectors to screen members. "The first purpose we have to solve is this informants business," one Grand Dragon announced. "We have to fight the FBI first. Then we can start on other goals."

Klan leaders tried to put the best light on their obvious problems. In 1971, Imperial Wizard Shelton launched a recruiting drive, but he disclaimed any need to rebuild. "The Klan has never degenerated," he boasted. "When the need has arisen, the Klan has always been there."

Despite the Klan's continued weakness, it still makes headlines. Its 100-year history of hooded terrorism guarantees press coverage for anyone claiming to speak for the Klan, and there are many would-be Wizards and Dragons competing for the limelight today. Robert Shelton, Imperial Wizard of the United Klans of America, continues to lead the largest group in Klandom, as he has since 1961. The second largest faction, the National Knights of the Ku Klux Klan, is headed by Imperial Wizard James Venable, an aging Georgian who has been a Klansman since the 1920s. The many other Klan leaders speak for groups so small that they could almost hold a Klonvocation in a telephone booth. Yet they easily get publicity because of the popular interest generated by the Invisible Empire.

As in other periods of weakness, Klan spokesmen have tried to give the order a new image in the 1970s. Restraint and moderation have become fashionable. Klansmen sporting coats and ties claim their society is prowhite, not antiblack. Klan rallies are open to newsmen. The traditional cross burning is referred to as a "cross lighting." Wash-

and-wear robes have been introduced. In the search for new members, Klan leaders emphasize quality and not quantity. "The days of taking in anyone who had the initiation fee are over," one Grand Dragon declares. Confirming the new line, Imperial Wizard Shelton has announced, "We're not interested so much in masses of people, but in the type that can give us leadership capacity."

A good example of the new-styled Klan leader is David E. Duke. As a recent graduate of Louisiana State University, Duke stands out in a group that has been notorious for attracting dropouts. With his well-spoken and polished manner, Duke has shown a flair for getting national, even international, recognition. The publicity-minded young man has been featured in newspapers and magazines. He's also a favorite on the college lecture circuit. However, Duke has been more successful at public relations than at recruiting. Although often referred to in the press as "national KKK director," Duke is actually the self-proclaimed leader of the "Knights of the Ku Klux Klan," a tiny splinter group in Louisiana. Indeed, when Duke staged a recent publicity stunt by supposedly creating a "Klan Border Watch" to keep illegal aliens out of the United States, more reporters showed up than Klansmen. Yet the desired result—extensive publicity—was achieved with a picture story in *Newsweek* magazine. Duke's success in getting publicity has angered rival Klansmen. "It amazes me how the media can accept his statements," complains Louisiana's Grand Dragon for a competing Klan. "David Duke doesn't get along with any Klan. Not a one. He recognizes no one and no one recognizes him." Robert Shelton dismisses Duke's group as a mail-order Klan that anyone may join.

Despite all the talk about a new image, the Klan message remains the same. Differences in style cannot conceal the antiblack, anti-Jewish, and anti-Catholic prejudice that dominates the Klan. Although Klansmen claim they are not a "bunch of niggerhaters," they openly attack people "with black skins and big lips." Indeed, most Klansmen still favor racial segregation. "People of the white and black races should be kept separate," Imperial Wizard Robert Shelton tells audiences. This is supposedly the result of belief in "racial pride," but the real reason was bluntly expressed by a would-be Klan poet.

> Black is beautiful,
> Tan is grand;
> But white is the color
> Of the big boss man.

The Klan's concern with race is so great that some groups have relaxed the old ban on Roman Catholics becoming members. However, Catholic spokesmen have warned that Klan membership is incompatible with the Catholic faith.

The Klan vents its religious hatred on Jews. "The Jews are the anti-Christ!" shouts Imperial Wizard Shelton at rallies. Shelton has also expressed support for anti-Israeli terrorists in the Mideast. "So what's wrong with the Arabs killing a few people to protect their land?" he asks.

Ultimately, Robert Shelton sees Communism as the root cause of America's problems. "The racial issue is a diversionary tactic to drive the country apart," he argues. "Communist influence has infiltrated the country so much that when the Communists decide to take over they won't have to fire a shot." For this reason the Imperial Wizard criticizes the metric system, saying, "It would make it much easier for the Communists when the takeover comes."

Clearly, the Klan's message, like its white hoods and robes, has changed little. Referring to recent efforts to clean up the Klan's image, David Duke once frankly admitted, "It's all window dressing, the substance is still the same." The Klan still appeals to racial and religious prejudice to explain away whatever causes discontent. Today, rising prices and unemployment trouble many Americans, and Klansmen are quick to exploit the resulting fears.

"The Klan is the type of organization that grows and decreases in cycles," explains one spokesman. "The cycle now is inflation, unemployment, crime. You've got everything the Klan can grow on today. You go to a small town and people are out of work. The mood is restless. They'll grasp the first thing that can help." Robert Shelton claims that the deportation of illegal aliens would eliminate unemployment. In this appeal to anti-immigrant feelings, Shelton overlooks the fact that most illegal aliens, especially Mexicans and other Latins, hold unskilled low paying jobs that few Americans would accept.

In addition to economic problems, the Klan has found a natural issue in government programs to aid minorities, particularly blacks. The order rails against both court-ordered busing to integrate schools and affirmative action programs to hire more blacks. Florida's Grand Dragon is frank to admit that the Klan's opposition to such policies is based on race. "I'm not against busing," he says candidly. "I rode a bus when I went to school. I'm against integration. The average man who say he's against busing is against integration. If he doesn't think so, he's not being honest."

The Klan's negativism makes it easy to exploit popular fears. "We don't have to go out looking for members of the Klan," boasts Robert Shelton. "Jimmy Carter and the government are bringing the people to us because of their practices."

After the violence of the 1960s, the Klan today emphasizes peaceful methods to achieve its goals. "We're trying to combat the liberal-media image of night-riding murderers," says Florida's Grand Dragon. "People are looking for some type of leadership to fight high crime, high inflation, busing, integration, dope, murders and permissiveness, and we think the Klan can provide it." As part of the new soft sell, some Klansmen have even suggested moving their rallies indoors to attract a better class of people. "We're trying to make it so if a man has a Cadillac automobile or a nice suit he won't have to go to a cow pasture to meet with us," Louisiana's Grand Dragon observes. However, faithful Klansmen show little liking for indoor rallies. "I'd rather be out in the free air in a pasture," says Robert Shelton. "I love the aroma of an open-air rally. And you can't have cross burning in a banquet hall."

Highly visible Klansmen have also taken their message to the streets. They appear in white robes and hoods, but unmasked to abide by antimask laws. In small-town shopping centers, uniformed Klansmen pass out literature and membership applications. On several occasions, Klansmen have staged marches through cities like Tallahassee and Lakeland, Florida. Hooded pickets have also protested in front of X-rated movie theaters and adult book shops.

As part of its new image, the KKK has resorted to lawsuits to fight court-ordered busing. In both Louisville, Kentucky, and Tampa, Florida, angry white parents recently filed lawsuits drawn up by Klan lawyers to stop further busing of children. Explaining his

114

cooperation with the Klan, one parent said the group "was the only one who presented a plan that could help us, and I'm willing to listen if someone has a better idea." In Tampa, protesting parents were accompanied to the federal courthouse by Imperial Wizard Shelton, who wore a business suit for the occasion. "People think we're a bunch of ignorant rednecks who can't read or write," commented Florida's Grand Dragon. "But I know people who can and they're willing to help." However, the federal courts dismissed the lawsuits.

In spite of all its image building and national publicity, the Klan has failed to attract many followers. Nevertheless, some leaders continue to make outrageous claims about the number of Klansmen today. Imperial Wizard James Venable, head of the National Knights of the Ku Klux Klan, routinely boasts of over a quarter of a million followers. Rather than make such ridiculous statements, most Klan leaders prefer to invoke the code of secrecy, refusing to talk about numbers. However, secrecy masks weakness, not strength. There are still some fifteen rival Klans, with feuds constantly leading to the creation of new ones. The smallest are one-man operations that exist only on paper. The largest are lucky if they attract several hundred people to their outdoor rallies, and that includes curious onlookers as well as dues-paying members and sympathizers.

After declining steadily, the various Klans reached their lowest point in the mid-1970s, when the FBI estimated their combined membership at 1,700. Since then, Klan fortunes have been on the upswing. Yet the FBI last reported that there are only 2,200 Klansmen in the country. Some observers contend that FBI estimates are too low, but whatever the exact number of Klansmen, the Invisible Empire is today a mere shadow of its former strength.

Klansmen are rarely found outside the South. There are a few isolated Klaverns in the midwestern states of Indiana and Ohio and in northeastern states like New Jersey, but they are small and ineffective. After the order suddenly reappeared in Illinois, the state legislature investigated the group and found only about 100 members spread among three Klan factions in 1976. "The Klan of today belongs in a comic strip," Illinois investigators concluded, "for there is indeed something amusing about a handful of grown men running around in white robes, burning crosses at picnics, who are unable to see that the issues that once attracted a large following—white supremacy, the red terror—are almost as dead as the Klan itself."

The Klan's history and its present weakness prevent it from having any political impact. Klansmen who have recently run for public office have failed miserably. Florida's Grand Dragon could not even get elected to a local school board. The Invisible Empire is so hated in most parts of the country, including the South, that its endorsement would be the kiss of death for any political candidate. The Grand Dragon of the Indiana Klan admitted that the KKK did not dare become openly identified with any politician it supported. "Until we're stronger, it might do more harm than good," he explained.

With the fall in membership has gone a noticeable decline in the violence related to the Klan. Yet there are constant reminders of the Klan's night-riding tradition. Although cross burnings designed as threats are illegal in most states, the flaming symbols of the Klan nonetheless mysteriously appear on occasion. The perpetrators are rarely caught. Klan rallies feature armed security guards with helmets and gray uniforms that make them look like Nazi storm troopers. Many spectators at Klan rallies openly flaunt firearms, including pistols and shotguns. Klan rhetoric still contains threats of violence. Imperial Wizard Robert Sheldon tells Klansmen that whites might have to use vigilante tactics in order to protect themselves against "the Negroes who are ravishing the towns, robbing and stabbing people." David Duke's clean-cut image was recently tarnished by his conviction for inciting to riot at a 1976 Klan rally. Duke is appealing the conviction and six-month jail sentence. Other Klan officials use a calling card that warns: "You have been paid a friendly visit by the Ku Klux Klan. Should we pay you a real visit?"

Such threats are still very real. In the early 1970s, a group of Michigan Klansmen engaged in a wave of violence directed against busing for integration. Five Knights, including a former Grand Dragon of the United Klans of America, were convicted of tarring and feathering a school principal and bombing school buses. More recently, several Florida Klansmen were charged with flogging a man. The persistence of such terrorist activities has made it difficult for Klansmen to recruit the "quality" people they talk about. Indeed, the Klan's reputation for violence drove the Imperial Wizard of a small splinter group, the Texas Fiery Knights, to resign. He found that even fellow

116

Klansmen were afraid to give him a job. "Most people, when you mention the KKK, think of terrorism, night-riding, burning and lynching, and this affects the image of all Klansmen," the former Imperial Wizard complained. "It ruins a man's reputation in the community."

Klansmen have also become the targets of violence. When 100 robed Knights staged a march through Tallahassee in 1977, they were taunted by anti-Klan demonstrators, one of whom hit a Klansman with a brick. A July 4 Klan rally on the steps of Ohio's state capitol was broken up by fist-swinging protestors who yelled, "Ku Klux Klan, scum of the land." Prevented from speaking, the humiliated Imperial Wizard of Ohio declared afterward: "The Klan will fight. We will kill. We have to rebuild." When he tried to hold a follow-up rally with some twenty Klansmen several months later, over 1,000 anti-Klan protestors also showed up. The rally ended with fistfights and a dozen arrests. At about the same time, a white Georgian broke up a Klan rally in President Jimmy Carter's hometown of Plains by driving a car into the speaker's platform. Although no one was seriously hurt, the assault charges drew a stiff twelve-year prison sentence for the protestor.

A highly publicized example of anti-Klan violence occurred in a Marine Corps barracks at Camp Pendleton, California. There, a group of black marines beat up seven white marines in the mistaken belief they were Klansmen. As it turned out, the real Klansmen were meeting in an adjoining room, where officers uncovered a secret cache of Klan literature, weapons, and a Klan membership list of sixteen marines. Several of the black marines complained that they had been beaten by the Klansmen, but Marine Corps officers charged the blacks with assault and simply reassigned the admitted Klansmen.

The aura of secrecy and violence surrounding the Invisible Empire shows why it must be taken seriously even though it now appears little more than a joke or nuisance. The Ku Klux Klan, whatever form it takes, will always pose a threat. Its infamous past guarantees that it will attract angry and frustrated people who turn to it as a last resort. Masked by white robes and hoods, they can vent their frustrations by cursing blacks, Jews, Catholics, and Communists, all of whom serve as convenient scapegoats for real problems like unemployment. Finally, the hatred aroused by the Klan can easily spill over into violence, as it so often has during the past hundred years.

"Klansmen now realize that you can be convicted for bombing and killing," a close observer of the KKK points out. "It's slowed them up, I think, but they'll always be a problem. You never know when four or five of this group are going to get all liquored up and pull something."

Glossary of Klan Terms

DOMAIN: A Klan unit made up of several state organizations (Realms).

EMPEROR: An honorary title created for William Joseph Simmons.

EXALTED CYCLOPS: The president of a local Klan chapter (Klavern).

GRAND: Refers to any state officer of the Klan, such as "Grand Klaliff."

GRAND DRAGON: The Klan official in charge of an entire state (Realm).

GRAND GOBLIN: A regional director in charge of a Domain.

GRAND WIZARD: A title, equivalent to Imperial Wizard, used by some leaders of splinter Klans after 1945.

IMPERIAL: Refers to any national officer or agency of the Klan, such as "Imperial Klabee."

IMPERIAL KLEAGLE: The national officer in charge of recruiting.

IMPERIAL PALACE: National Klan headquarters in Atlanta during the 1920s and 1930s.

IMPERIAL WIZARD: The highest Klan official.

INVISIBLE EMPIRE: Refers to both the administrative structure of the Klan and its entire membership.

KING KLEAGLE: The state officer in charge of recruiting.

KLABEE: The treasurer of a local Klan chapter.

KLALIFF: The vice-president of a local Klan chapter.

KLANISHNESS: The group feeling shared by Klansmen.

KLANKRAFT: Klan rituals.

KLANKREST: The Atlanta home of the Imperial Wizard during the 1920s and 1930s.

KLANSMAN: A member of the Klan.

KLANSWOMAN: A member of the Women of the Ku Klux Klan.

KLAVERN: A local chapter of the Klan and its meeting place.

KLEAGLE: A recruiter for the Klan.

KLECTOKEN: The Klan's initiation fee.

KLIGRAPP: The secretary of a local Klan chapter.

KLOKANN: The executive committee of a local Klan chapter, composed of local officers.

KLOKARD: A Klan lecturer.

KLONCILIUM: An executive committee of the Klan.

KLONVERSATION: A Klan conversation in secret code.

KLONVOCATION: A national convention of the Klan.

KLORAN: The book of Klan ritual created by William Joseph Simmons.

KLORERO: A state convention of the Klan.

KLUDD: The chaplain of a local Klan chapter.

KNIGHT: A Klan member; used interchangeably with Klansman.

KONKLAVE: A meeting of Klansmen.

NATURALIZATION: The initiation ceremony for new Klan members.

NIGHT HAWK: An official responsible for Klan investigations.

REALM: A Klan unit equivalent to a state.

WOMEN OF THE KU KLUX KLAN: An auxiliary of the Klan created for women, who were barred from full membership in the Klan.

Selected Bibliography

Alexander, Charles C. *The Ku Klux Klan in the Southwest.* Lexington: University of Kentucky Press, 1965.

Chalmers, David. *Hooded Americanism: The History of the Ku Klux Klan.* Chicago: Quadrangle, 1968.

Coughlan, Robert. "Konklave in Kokomo." *The Aspirin Age, 1919–1941.* Ed. Isabel Leighton. New York: Simon and Schuster, 1949.

Craven, Charles. "The Robeson County Indian Uprising against the KKK." *South Atlantic Quarterly* 57 (Autumn, 1958), pp. 433–42.

Degler, Carl N. "A Century of the Klans: A Review Article." *Journal of Southern History* 31 (November, 1965), pp. 435–43.

Frost, Stanley. *The Challenge of the Klan.* Indianapolis, Ind.: Bobbs-Merrill, 1924.

Fry, Henry P. *The Modern Ku Klux Klan.* Boston: Small, Maynard, 1922.

Hamilton, Virginia Van der Veer. *Hugo Black: The Alabama Years.* Baton Rouge: Louisiana State University, 1972.

Harrell, Kenneth Earl. "The Ku Klux Klan in Louisiana, 1920–1930." Ph.D. dissertation, Louisiana State University, 1966.

Huie, William Bradford. *Three Lives for Mississippi.* New York: WCC Books, 1965.

Jackson, Kenneth T. *The Ku Klux Klan in the City, 1915–1930.* New York: Oxford University Press, 1967.

Kennedy, Stetson. *I Rode with the Ku Klux Klan.* London: Arco, 1954.

Kourier, 1932–1936.

Loucks, Emerson H. *The Ku Klux Klan in Pennsylvania: A Study in Nativism.* Harrisburg, Pa.: Telegraph Press, 1936.

Mecklin, John Moffatt. *The Ku Klux Klan: A Study of the American Mind.* New York: Russell & Russell, 1924.

Randel, William Peirce. *The Ku Klux Klan: A Century of Infamy.* Philadelphia: Chilton, 1965.

Rice, Arnold S. *The Ku Klux Klan in American Politics.* Washington, D.C.: Haskell, 1962.

Trelease, Allen W. *White Terror: The Ku Klux Klan Conspiracy and Southern Reconstruction.* New York: Harper & Row, 1971.

U.S. Congress. House Committee on Rules. *The Ku-Klux Klan: Hearings.* 67th Cong., 1st sess., 1921.

————. Committee on Un-American Activities. *The Present-Day Ku Klux Klan Movement.* Washington, D.C.: Government Printing Office, 1967.

Weaver, Norman F. "The Knights of the Ku Klux Klan in Wisconsin, Indiana, Ohio, and Michigan." Ph.D. dissertation, University of Wisconsin, 1954.

Whitehead, Don. *Attack on Terror: The FBI against the Ku Klux Klan in Mississippi.* New York: Funk & Wagnalls, 1970.

Index